Only Through Grace...

By
Charles Smith and Reverend Jerry Ross

authorHOUSE®

AuthorHouse™
1663 Liberty Drive, Suite 200
Bloomington, IN 47403
www.authorhouse.com
Phone: 1-800-839-8640

© 2009 The Jerry Ross Story as told to Charles Smith. All rights reserved.

*No part of this book may be reproduced, stored in a retrieval system, or
transmitted by any means without the written permission of the author.*

First published by AuthorHouse 4/28/2009

ISBN: 978-1-4389-7519-1 (sc)
ISBN: 978-1-4389-7520-7 (hc)

Printed in the United States of America
Bloomington, Indiana

This book is printed on acid-free paper.

PROLOGUE

Grace, love, fear, denial, miracle, and commitment are words that are familiar to each of us. They have a special meaning in the life of Jerry Ross. He has experienced each of them to the fullest extent of meaning during various periods of his life from childhood to mature adulthood. This book is a chronicle of Jerry Ross's life as he has struggled with the challenges of growing up and finding his place of service in a troubled world.

Jerry was born and raised near Boaz, Alabama on the Sand Mountain plateau. This area is a part of the southeastern part of the United States commonly known as the "Bible Belt." Coming from a God-fearing family, he was raised by Christian parents who desired the same type of life for Jerry and his siblings. The commitment to God, family, others, and country were the baseline principles of their lives. These principles were instilled in Jerry at an early age—but he refused to believe and live by them.

Jerry's life has evolved through several stages, beginning with his early teenage years. During those years (the early to mid 1960s), he went through a period of denial and rebellion, during which he began his flight from the acceptance of God and His calling. While knowing deep within that a living God of Love existed, Jerry outwardly denied the existence of God. Filled with the exuberance of youth and as a member of the "beat" generation, he felt that he was sufficient within himself to face the challenges thrown at him by a troubled world and society.

His entrance into the military started a period of change of mind and attitude for Ross. The Viet Nam War, a very unpopular action, presented many challenges to him. Jerry was drafted into the military service in the mid 1960s. He received his basic training as an infantryman and shortly thereafter was given orders to report for service in the Vietnam conflict. In this period of overseas wartime duty, Jerry distinguished himself with his valor, heroism under enemy fire, and concern for the safety of his fellow military associates and members of the South Vietnamese armed forces. Specialist Ross received several decorations for going beyond the call of duty. During this period of turmoil and danger brushes with death in the heat of fierce battles with a determined enemy. With death all around him, he began to wonder about why he was spared. Slowly but surely, Jerry began to realize that the hand of God had protected him. He began to recognize that a special thing was happening in his life and that perhaps there was indeed a God of mercy, love, and compassion.

Following military duty, Jerry Ross returned to civilian life. Although God was dealing with him, he was still in denial about accepting Christianity as a way of life. He felt that he was sufficient in himself to meet the challenges of life. After a time of running from God, conviction became his constant companion. Many devoted Christians were offering prayers on his behalf and were displaying a genuine interest in seeing a positive change in his life. After a period of time, all of those efforts paid off; Jerry received Christ into his life. This was the first of many glorious experiences with God.

Following that monumental event, Ross became active on the battlefield of life. He began to serve in the church and eventually answered the call into God's ministry. He has served in several areas of church work, including pastoral work. The experiences in the Christian period of his life have served to deepen his understanding of God's purpose for his life, and have given him a bedrock desire to tell the story of Jesus and His love. Jerry is quick to give credit to God for any his accomplishments and steadfastly refuses to take any credit for himself.

Jerry Ross's experiences in combat were perhaps the beginning of a realization that God was dealing with him and was protecting him in times of intense enemy gunfire. Working in God's field has broadened

A Brief Statement from

Reverend Jerry Ross

First of all, I'd like thank the members of my immediate family for their love and tireless support during the preparation of this book My wife Darlene has been a pillar of strength the whole time and a great source of eyewitness information, particularly in the areas of our church work and during my lengthy hospitalization following my near-fatal heart attack. Our sons, Daryl (and his wife Cresap) and Shane (and his wife Dawn), have provided help and support in many ways, not the least of which has been moral support. Daryl and Cresap's sons, Tyler and Avery, and Shane and Dawn's daughter, Madisyn, have been a source of joy during this project. I am doubly blessed because both of our sons are ministers of God's Word.

I want to thank everybody, and I know that a lot of them would have liked to have their names put in the book. Let me start by saying that if I tried to put the names of all the people who have been an influence and help in my life in this book, it would be impossible to list them all, because the list is so long. A great number of people in all the congregations I have been privileged to serve have shown great love and untiring support for my family and me during my time with them. So many people, including a large number of family members, have bent over backwards to help me

ix

get saved by the grace of God. Then, after I was saved, these same people helped me to humble myself enough to yield to the calling of the Lord. After that, they helped me learn to study the Bible, pray for God's guidance, and then follow that guidance and the example, help, and influence of those saints of God. Most importantly, they taught me to put God and His Word first as I tried to sort out the situations and problems that occurred in my life, and to verify which way God wanted me go in dealing with them. They also taught me to always put the advice of mankind in second place when doing God's work.

I want to thank all the people who reached out to me during my life, especially those in my pastorates and other churches, along with those elderly saints of God. During my ministry, I was blessed to be able to get out and visit with the dear people in the hospitals and nursing homes. It was a joy to me—a young and healthy preacher at the time—to see those dedicated servants of God, some of them seventy or eighty years old, still going strong and active with their witnessing and work in God's field. What a blessing it was to see those people still telling someone about the Lord and trying to get sinners saved after many years of service to God. They were telling others that Jesus was right for whatever was wrong in their lives and that they needed Him in their lives to fix those erring ways.

I went to the Word of God to find help when I went out into the fields, highways, and byways trying to compel people to come to the Lord. During those times, I found many different philosophies concerning the act of getting saved. Many of those unsaved people had strange ideas and concepts about the process of salvation. They would say, "You can't get saved for this" or "You can't be saved because of that." Many of those philosophies, as formulated and modified by mankind, went far astray from God's plan of salvation and proved to be a detriment to people's lives. I turned to the third chapter of the book of John (a most familiar passage) for help in explaining the good news of the gospel to lost people. That chapter explains God's love for sinners and the price that was paid for the simple plan He provides for salvation. The words of Jesus Christ as he explains God's plan are in red. Christ said in that passage of scripture, "And as Moses lifted up the serpent in the wilderness, even so must the Son of Man be lifted up: that whosoever believeth in him should not perish, but have eternal life. For God so loved the world, that he gave his only begotten Son, that whosoever believeth in Him should not perish, but have eternal life." Jesus also said in John 12:32, "And I, if I be lifted up from the earth, will draw all men unto me." That includes you and me.

In the book of Romans, after the death of the Lord Jesus Christ, Paul began to preach the message of Christ to the Romans and to other gentile groups. Those people knew Paul as an intelligent person in the faith they were walking in as he came preaching the new doctrine. Lots of them wanted to hear him as he went about preaching. At the same time, Peter was preaching to the Jewish Christians, delivering the same doctrine as Paul. Although Paul and Peter were ministering to groups that had differing philosophies concerning religion, each of them faced strong opposition from some members of the groups that they were serving at the time because of the new doctrine that they were preaching.

I thought of Paul and Peter when I began to walk with the Lord. I found that everything that the Lord laid on my heart for me to do did not always agree with tradition. Like them, I found that there were times when I faced opposition to my ministry because of the influence of past practices and traditions in the church. But now, it has come time in my life when I feel that God is in this work with me and Brother Charles. I want to thank him and his family for their help in this project and for his time and effort in this.

It has come time for me to try to show people that anything that is done or accomplished in this life is not because of the wisdom of the head, but it is because of the guidance and leadership of God and obedience to Him. Anything we do should bring glory to God. That is the reason that I know that God led me, not just me but us, to name the book Only Through Grace.

If you will sit down and read this book, we hope and pray that it will touch your heart in some way. If it does touch you and lead you into a closer relationship with Him, then we will feel that we have done the things He wanted us to do in this project. In other words, we have reached our goal. We will feel that we have done the thing God commissioned us to do with this book. I praise Him to the highest for His help and guidance in this work and for His protecting hand, love, and patience that have overshadowed me all my life. I give Him the glory for it all.

I want to say a heartfelt thank you to every person or group mentioned in this book. Without your help and support through the years, none of this would have been possible. I am proud that each of you is a part of my life. I pray that you will continue to help me and pray for me as we work together in His field, but most of all, I want you to know that I love you, appreciate you, and thank God for you. God bless you.

CHAPTER 1

THE EARLY YEARS

The Jerry Ross story has its beginning in the Sand Mountain area of northeast Alabama. The Sand Mountain area is in the middle of the Bible Belt of the southeastern section of the United States. It is an area filled with people who thrive on church activities and service to the loving God of Creation. It is also an area that has a rich history of gospel singing, dinner on the grounds, and sharing and helping others. The Sand Mountain plateau, formerly an area with a thriving agrarian economy, has changed with the times and is now recognized as a manufacturing and retail sales leader and considered to be the nation's most densely populated rural area.

A native of Etowah County, Alabama, Ross was born into this environment in 1945. Jerry's parents, Hermus and Ruby Ross, were hardworking, churchgoing people who believed in the Bible and who taught its principles to their children. The Ross children were taught the value of a Christian life and the benefits of regular church attendance. Mrs. Ruby Ross, a dedicated Christian lady, was a very definite influence in Jerry's life in his early formative years, even though he did little to acknowledge it. She taught her children by word of mouth, by sharing the teachings of the Bible, and by her own living example and testimony. Jerry was exposed to that atmosphere and philosophy from the earliest times of his life. In those times, however, he took a more or less passive interest in church and was—at best—a skeptical believer in Christ.

During those most important formative years, Jerry attended Pleasant Hill Southern Baptist Church near Boaz, Alabama. Pleasant Hill Church was and is a typical county church where the gospel is preached and taught in its purity with a great deal of spirit and power. Powerful sermons by the Reverend Harvey Stewart and others fell on his ears but did not settle in his heart. He realizes now that while the seeds of a life of Christian service and dedication were being planted at that time, the seeds were very slow to germinate because of his indifference to the call of the Holy Spirit and his resistance to the meaning of the messages being sent his way.

Sunday school and church were a vital part of the Ross children's lives in the childhood years. Their mother Ruby was a strict disciplinarian with strong faith and a solid grounding in Christian living. Attending Sunday school and church were a mandate by Mrs. Ross, one that was firmly enforced. Jerry states today that his mother was an inspiration to him in that time and that she did her best to nurture him in the development of a healthy and committed Christian life.

Another realm of Christian influence also played a part in God's plan to bring Jerry Ross into the Christian fold of workers and believers. Local radio stations began to appear on the scene in the late 1940s. Most of those stations offered gospel programming that included gospel singing by local groups and preaching by local evangelists. That practice was prevalent in the 1950s and 1960s, and it continues to the present time. As a teenager, Jerry was impressed by two local radio evangelists, the Reverend Raymond Cook and the Reverend J. P. Rowan. These two men pastored local churches and created personal radio ministries that still continue. Although, once again, seeds were being planted in Jerry's heart, he rejected them at the time and did nothing to allow them to sprout and bring forth fruit.

Jerry attended Sardis, Alabama schools that were a part of the Etowah County School System. He participated in all the usual school activities—sports, peer group activities, and other programs of interest to him and his age group. Although he had the ability to be an outstanding student, he was never really challenged to pursue excellence in all phases of his schoolwork, particularly in reading and the arts. By his own evaluation of his schoolwork, he was an average student, but one with better-than-average grades. In the lower grades, he was blessed with the ability to make good grades with very little work and without carrying books home at night. He relied on a great memory and the ability to listen in class to achieve good grades and standing in his class.

Even though he was a straight-A student for his early years in school, he developed the bad habit of cheating on his work. One of his teachers, Mrs. Norris (who was his mother's double first cousin and who bore a striking resemblance to Jerry's mother), arranged for him to be in her class at the Sardis School. She dealt very forthrightly with his propensity to cheat. She kept him in the classroom one day during a break for recess. During this time, she talked very sternly with him and explained about the finer points of education, studying, and paying attention in class. She punctuated her stern lecture by asking him to bend over and grasp his ankles. She then applied the "board of education" with considerable vigor. With this incentive, his grades improved for the rest of his elementary school career, but slipped again as he moved into junior high school in the seventh grade.

Ross fully and clearly realizes now that he made a mistake at that time of his life. Instead of going the way of the world at that time, he wishes now that he had remained with the group of students who persevered through high school and were nurtured by outstanding and dedicated Christian teachers. He and some of his contemporaries felt at the time that those students who listened to parents and teachers were weak and unable to act on their own. It is more than obvious to Ross now that he missed a great opportunity to learn something of a great philosophy of life and what Christian living was all about.

Intramural sports were of great interest to him in his school years. He was pushed by a desire to excel and to win. These characteristics were to appear again in later life, when he was a soldier in the United States Army, and yet another time, after he converted to Christianity. As time went by in his school years, he began to be influenced by a new culture appearing among many people of all ages in the United States. The culture of "doing your own thing," "taking care of number one," and "doing what feels good" seemed very enticing to Jerry. The "in" thing at the time was to be in the clique of young people sharing that culture. This eventually led to his quitting school after the eleventh grade.

3

His outlook on life began to change at that time; things of the world began to attract his attention and influence his thinking. Although he had been brought up in church, he began to drift away from church and the Christian way of living. He developed a strong conviction that he did not need church; as a result, he drifted away from the church more and more each day. Jerry was guided by the erroneous principle that if a person wanted to be a big man, it was better to go the "rough" way, rather than the Christian way. He felt that this would get more recognition. He now believes that young people of that time (and indeed, even now) craved attention and would do whatever it took to get it. In those early and formative teenage years, Jerry started to have serious doubts about living a Christian life. Outwardly, he began to reject any commitment to living a Christian life. Feeling that he would have to go the rough way to accomplish his goals in life, Jerry began to develop a hard and cold attitude toward church at this time. He began to observe church members in their daily lives and as they worshipped in their churches. He was not interested in the good things that happened in the lives of dedicated Christians and the good works performed by them. Rather, he looked for mistakes in those lives and openly gloated over those failures and setbacks. That attitude and demeanor led Jerry further and further from a Christian life. Even in that period, however, there was still a spark inside Jerry's heart that was burning—albeit in a very small way. Despite his efforts to squelch it, the spark still glowed as God continued to fuel it. Ross now knows and has confessed that God was dealing with him at the time. Although he tried in a very determined manner, he was never able to completely extinguish the spark and push God completely out of his life. He now knows and firmly believes that once a sinner hears the Word and God begins to deal with him or her, that person will always remember God's knock on his or her heart's door.

This philosophy and the influence of teenage culture at the time gained a stronger hold on him; this caused him to quit going to church at the age of thirteen or fourteen. He began to proclaim, sometimes loudly, that he "didn't need the church" and that there was nothing to "this thing of giving one's life to Christ and living for Him." Moving into this new phase of his life, he began to live a very worldly life; he got further and further from living the Christian life his mother and family desired for him.

Of the nine children born to Hermos and Ruby Ross, eight were raised to adulthood by the dedicated Christian parents. One of the Ross children died at the age of eighteen months. Ruby Ross had a burden for her children to be converted to Christianity; she did the things only a loving mother could do for her children. Weekends were reserved for the honoring and worshiping of a living God by the parents and the Ross children. On any day of the week, with particular emphasis on Sundays, Ruby Ross would tune the family radio to local stations broadcasting gospel programming and turn the volume up so everyone in the house could hear it. She would prepare for church and the Sunday meal as she worked and listened to gospel music and preaching. At times, she would break forth in song, singing some old hymns such as "How Beautiful Heaven Must Be" or "Amazing Grace." During some of those experiences, Ruby Ross felt the spirit of God so strongly that she would break forth in a shout of praise to God. Her children did not realize at the time that she was carrying a Christian mother's burden for her lost children. Those Sunday mornings were particularly agonizing for Jerry. Many times on those days, he would be suffering the throes of a hangover throughout his physical body and the tragedy of a war between the forces of good and evil going on in his spiritual body. During that period of his life, he was putting up the outward appearance of a tough, worldly man, while on the inside he was secretly resisting and pushing God aside. Although Jerry did not realize it at the time, he now knows that God's plan for his life was being developed at that time.

As the end of Jerry Ross's eleventh year of formal schooling approached, he dropped out of school and began to take part in the activities of the secular world and the so-called "seamy" side of life. After leaving school, he looked for a job and soon found one that was to his liking. It supplied a teenaged young man with enough money to indulge in the things and activities of the crude and rowdy type of life. Jerry's first job was at a business called Whorton's Truck Farm of Mountainboro, Alabama. Whorton's was a firm that dealt in used parts for trucks of all types. The main job duty for Ross was the removal, cataloging, storing, and selling of used truck parts. As a part of his job at that time, he was responsible for going to Chicago or Detroit every other weekend to pick up damaged vehicles and returning them to Mountainboro to salvage the parts. These trips served another bad purpose in Jerry's life: They showed him a snapshot of

5

nightlife and other questionable activities in those towns and surrounding areas that were "of the world" and as such, were an extremely bad influence on a young person experiencing them for the first time.

Jerry had a desire to test his wings as he participated in the secular things and activities that were an integral part of the rougher type of life. He desperately sought recognition for himself as a full-fledged member of the rebellious groups of teenagers so prevalent at that time. He wanted to show the world that he was a tough guy—and one who was able to make it on his own. A partying lifestyle was his desire and goal in those days. His was a life dominated by the three Ws: wine, women, and whiskey.

As time went by, Jerry became even more involved in the day-to-day activities of his chosen lifestyle. Even as he fully embraced his newfound way of life and became heavily involved in it, God continued to quietly work with him, particularly after episodes of raucous and wild parties that he enjoyed so much. Even though he thought he was enjoying the activities of the seamier side of life, those parties had their bad effect on Jerry; they began to take a heavy toll on him. He found it harder and harder to face new days as they came. It became far more difficult for him to fit into the society in which he lived, even into the Christian atmosphere of the Ross home. After many of these rowdy, late-night bouts of drinking and carousing, Jerry would awaken with splitting headaches and all the other symptoms of a hangover.

As the rigors of his chosen worldly lifestyle began to affect his health and life in many detrimental ways, Jerry began to consider the pathway he had chosen. He wondered if it was leading him in a direction to produce a meaningful life. He felt that the Spirit of God was dealing with him once again. During these times, Ross would awaken in the clutches of a hangover and secretly wish that someone would come to him and say, "Let's go find a preacher! Jerry, you need help now!" Feeling condemned when such thoughts would come to his mind, Jerry would keep them bottled up within. He would not consider sharing his deep spiritual needs with anyone. He continued to push God aside. He resisted the prodding of the Holy Spirit. Even with Jerry's misguided choice of living a worldly life, he says that God never ceased to work with him. It is his contention now that once the Spirit of God begins to deal with a person, it never completely leaves him. God—being the merciful and loving God that He is—continues to love his children even when they are living apart from Him. He wants them to come home. The life of Jerry Ross is the ideal example of how God's love for his sinful children and His patience and grace toward them continues to be expressed.

After working at Whorton's Truck Farm for about two and a half years, Jerry went to work with the Guntersville Spinning Mill. After working there for a period of time, the call of the North—with its secular and oftentimes sinful activities—began to appeal to Jerry Ross. Having friends who had moved to the North, he coveted the money, nightlife, and parties of that area that he had heard so much about. He convinced himself that Michigan was the place to be. He decided to move north and join those friends. He was enamored of the prospect of living his life in an atmosphere of parties, liquor, and rowdy friends. By his own statement, Jerry was entering a critical period of his life at this time. He considered himself to be completely in charge of his life and capable of calling his own shots when it came to living his life. He disdained any efforts—especially those of his parents—to control him. Unlike his brothers and sisters, Jerry was the "wild" one of the Ross brood. He strongly resisted the best efforts of his parents and siblings to help him turn his life around. During this time, wanderlust became a major factor in his life; he decided to quit his job near home and move to the northern United States.

Jerry left home and headed north to Flint, Michigan in search of money and good times. Arriving in Flint with little or no experience that would qualify him for work in that area, he put his gifted mind to work in seeking employment. He got into trouble in short order in Flint and quickly moved to Detroit—to leave the Flint problem behind. Being almost without funds and in need of a job, Jerry ventured forth looking for work. Jerry fancied himself a good talker and one who was able to present his case and hold his own regardless of the place, subject, or personality involved.

While pounding the streets of Detroit looking for a job, Jerry noticed a sign advertising for a machinist at the R. C. Mahon Machine Company. Without knowing a milling machine from a lathe or a drill press from a boring mill, he went into the plant and inquired about the machinist's job. During the interview, the personnel department employee determined very quickly that Jerry didn't know a thing about the machinist trade. Although he was terribly deficient in machining skills, he was long on audacity and the ability to talk and sell himself. In spite of his obvious lack of experience, a supervisor overheard the interview and Jerry was hired on the spot by the Mahon Company. The personnel employee hired him not because of any experience or qualification, but because he was, admittedly, a good talker who was very sure of himself and able to sell himself. Upon being hired, Jerry was assigned duties in the final finish area of the plant, where components of metal buildings were formed into final dimensions, coated or painted, and prepared for shipment. He operated items of equipment in this area as specified by union contract.

Up to and throughout this period of time, God continued to deal with Jerry. It is interesting to note that God had given Jerry other notable gifts: the gifts of salesmanship and leadership, as well as the ability to express himself clearly while communicating with other people. Even though Jerry didn't realize it at the time, God was preparing him for that day in the future when he would surrender himself to the Lord and accept His calling. Little did he know that he would need all of those skills to do the work God had in store for him in the future. He did not realize that God prepared those He had selected for special work.

While working for the R. C. Mahon Company, Jerry experienced an issue that would lead to a change in his life and would push him to the very limits of his capability before it ended. A letter from the Selective Service Department arrived, bringing greetings from his friends and fellow citizens. The letter advised him that he was to report for duty in the military service and gave specific instructions as to the place and time of reporting.

At first, Jerry considered having his records transferred to Detroit, hoping that he could prolong his status as a civilian by a period of at least six months by doing so. The second step of his plan was to move back to Alabama when the Michigan Selective Service got too hot on his trail. He felt that this would give him an additional six months of civilian life. He sought to be an artful draft dodger by exploring and utilizing every loophole in the Selective Service Law. Eventually, however, Jerry realized inside that he had a duty to serve his country, a duty that he, in good conscience, could not shirk. Another factor that influenced his decision not to contest induction into the armed forces of the country was his lifestyle while living in Detroit. He was participating in activities that could eventually place him in danger, possibly with consequences as serious as endangering his life.

This was a time in the life of a young Jerry Ross when he had no specific goals other than partying and having a good time. He had not thought much about marrying, settling down, raising a family, and building a future that would be beneficial to himself and pleasing to God.

At this crossroads of life, Jerry was still feeling turmoil inside as the Spirit of God and the forces of evil struggled to gain control of his life. He stated that from the time he was eight years old, when he first listened to powerful sermons until the time when he was eventually saved, he felt this warfare. Many witnesses said and did things during that time that were like lights to him. To his credit, he recognized even then that all of God's children are witnesses who can have an effect on sinners. Jerry acknowledges that many of those things shared with him in those days by determined witnesses found a lodging place in his heart. Unfortunately, he still continued to resist God's overtures and refused to acknowledge them to anyone.

Jerry Ross answered the call to serve his country with this inward conflict raging within his very being and the unpopular war in Vietnam facing him in the near future. The wonderful thing is that God—fully aware of Jerry's rebellious nature—continued to love him and protect him and prepare him for a future work.

CHAPTER 2

THE ARMY YEARS

The 1960s were a turbulent time for the United States and its citizens. Within the continental boundaries of the States, several major issues confronted the governmental agencies and created general unrest in the country. The decade saw the election of John F. Kennedy, the first Roman Catholic president of the United States, and the passage of the Civil Rights Act of 1964. These two events polarized the populace to a large degree.

During this decade, the Berlin Wall was erected, thereby creating major problems for the United States, France, and Great Britain. The wall stood until the time of President Ronald Reagan. In 1961, the highly unsuccessful Bay of Pigs incident occurred. Also in 1961, the Russians beat the United States into space by putting Cosmonaut Yuri Gagarin in orbit around the Earth. American astronaut John Glenn became the second man to orbit the Earth. His adventure took place in 1962.

The assassinations of several key leaders of the United States occurred during the 1960s: President John F. Kennedy was assassinated in Dallas, Texas on November 22, 1963; civil rights leader Martin Luther King, Jr. was assassinated in Memphis, Tennessee on April 4, 1968; and during a campaign stop in California on his campaign for president, United States Senator Robert Kennedy was assassinated by Sirhan Sirhan on June 6.

In the early 1960s, political unrest began to be a major issue in Vietnam, a country formerly known as French Indochina. Political factions succeeded in dividing the country into North Vietnam and South Vietnam. While the northern group was communistic in government, the south leaned toward democracy. North Vietnam—with support from communist countries to the north—sought to spread communism throughout that part of the world. Major democracies around the world realized that the spread of communism must be halted and forged plans to achieve that end.

Following the Gulf of Tonkin incident in 1964, the United States Congress passed a resolution giving President Lyndon Johnson the power to deploy troops without congressional approval. President Johnson exercised that authority, and by year's end in 1965, he had deployed 185,000 troops in Vietnam. This number was eventually increased to 540,000 by 1969. The whole issue created a considerable amount of political backlash throughout the country, particularly among student groups. Many demonstrations—some violent—were staged in several areas of this country. A notable event of this nature was the episode at Kent State University. The Vietnam War was viewed by many as an unpopular war and one that was totally wrong and being fought for the wrong reasons. This war also brought a change in the military aspect of the conflict. There were not clear lines of demarcation as in past wars. The Vietnam War saw the birth of true guerilla and terrorist warfare.

Jerry Ross was one of several hundred thousand who were drafted into the Armed Forces to fight the spread of communism on foreign soil without the wholehearted support of all Americans back home. Jerry rolled his personal situation over in his mind while trying to decide what was best for him and what would be the best path for him to travel. Although he considered ways to beat the draft when conscription became a certainty, Jerry re-evaluated his situation and began to get his priorities in the proper order. He slowly but surely realized that he owed a debt to his country, his family, and his community. Oddly enough, during this time, he felt God pricking his conscience once again. Jerry chose not to fight induction into the armed services and accepted the opportunity to serve his country. To their credit, several hundred thousand young people accepted the call to military service and set out to make a difference. Jerry and all his contemporaries chose to do their duty by meeting the enemy head on, rather than by shirking their duty and running and hiding from him in some other country. These brave souls deserve this country's highest respect and appreciation for their sacrifices. Let us not forget that tens of thousands of them made the supreme sacrifice.

At the time of his call-up, Jerry Ross was an employee of the R. C. Mahon Steel Company in Detroit, Michigan. By his own statement, he had a good job that provided him with good wages. He was a young, single man away from home and out from under the strict tutelage of Christian parents. He had become an active participant in many worldly things that were leading him down the path to heartache and ruin. In his own mind, he was bulletproof and ten feet tall while doing those things he knew to be wrong. At the time of receiving his summons from the Selective Service, Jerry told his employer that he would be back to work in a few days, probably in a week or less.

Jerry reported to the Selective Service Induction Center at Maxwell Air Force Base in Montgomery, Alabama. The induction process did not go according to plan for Ross. Although he felt he could beat the system and had tried several things he had heard of new recruits trying in their futile efforts to fail the physical exam, the system claimed him. He tried his best to fail the physical examination, but trying his best to fail, he passed the physical exam with flying colors. To his credit, he did not resort to swallowing aluminum foil to give indication of an ulcer, nor did he try other devious methods to give a false indication of a medical problem. He also did his best to fail the written test. In an effort to answer as many questions as possible and hopefully produce many wrong answers, he went through the test blindly marking answers without regard to question content and, in many cases, without any effort to derive a correct answer. He felt that he would be sure to fail while using his method, but wonder of wonders, he made a very high score on the tests. He now realizes and feels that God was dealing with him once again. He states today that he believes that God was in charge of his life, even though he was rebelling at the overtures of the His Spirit. Today, Jerry feels that God, in His infinite wisdom, sent him to Vietnam for a purpose. That purpose was to show him that, indeed, he could die and go to hell halfway around the world from his home in Boaz, Alabama if he did not get himself right with God. Little did Jerry realize that God was still being patient with him and was once again extending his marvelous grace to him.

Following the successful physical examination and high written test scores he achieved during his induction process, Jerry began to see the light, albeit dimly. He stated that, in view of his better-than-average scores, he was going to make the best of it and would do the utmost to come out of the situation alive. He decided to do his best in all of his training and conditioning activities and to learn everything he could to help improve his chances of survival in Vietnam. With this positive change of mind and attitude regarding his life, Jerry reported to Fort Gordon, Georgia for his basic training.

Basic training was a rude awakening for a young man who felt he was bulletproof and ten feet tall. Jerry, a young man who was accustomed to doing all things his own way and calling his own shots, was suddenly thrust into a situation where someone else was calling the shots. During the weeks of basic training, he learned the hard way that he had to do things as a tough drill sergeant told him. It was particularly galling to him to have to listen to someone yelling in his ear many hours every day. It was extremely hard for Jerry to be talked to in such a manner and not be able to talk back. The drill instructor and other members of his cadre tried to tell him that things could be worse, especially in combat. The training emphasized that he must be willing to take orders and carry them out as directed. Jerry was learning that the army way of doing things was quite different from the way he had done things as a civilian.

As the training progressed, however, Jerry Ross began to see the light. Reality set in. He knew that he was going to Vietnam after his training was completed. He knew that he was on the fast track to becoming a member of a combat team. With this realization, he resolved to learn all he could during his training and, by doing so, be better prepared to hopefully preserve his life while engaged in combat on the battlefield. He completed his basic training at Fort Gordon with a different outlook on life. Although he was still pushing God aside, Jerry began to fully realize that he was indeed mortal, and that being in battle could be a very dangerous proposition and one that was not conducive to long life.

The next step in Jerry's transformation was being shipped to Fort Jackson, South Carolina for advanced infantry training. The advanced infantry training took eight weeks and was a serious time of testing for Jerry and his fellow recruits. The real reason for being in the army was becoming obvious to those young men. They were to become well-trained and efficient fighting men who understood the credo of "kill or be killed." The distinct possibility of going to Vietnam loomed heavily like a dark storm cloud on the horizon, and the possibility of going was becoming more of a certainty as the days went by.

During this phase of his training, Jerry met a young man from Sweden who was a born-again Christian. The young man saw an opportunity to witness to Jerry about the plan of salvation. The young man's witness was so strong and to the point that Jerry began to think positively about God for a short time as the young Swede gave him the details of the plan of salvation. He became so interested in what was being said that he called his mother for the express purpose of getting her thoughts on the issue. He knew that she knew about denominations, Bible translations, and most of all, about the plan of salvation. After hearing Jerry's side of the story, she stated that the young man from Sweden seemed to her to be a true Christian young man and one who was worth listening to. Even though God was dealing with Jerry in a strong way at that time, he said that Satan planted the seeds of doubt in his mind at the time; he began to pull back from the association with the young man from Sweden.

In this time of great change and many uncertainties in his life, Jerry began to avoid close relationships with anyone. He felt that entering into a close, friendly relationship with anyone might reveal any inner weaknesses that he might have. In his own words, he became very hard-hearted during that period of his life. He did not fully trust any of his contemporaries or most of the other people around him. One thing in his favor, however, was the fact that he decided to make the most of his training and learn all he could about his new job as an infantryman in the United States Army. An ulterior motive in Jerry's mind at the time was self-preservation.

For the first time in his life, he put effort into learning all he could and doing his best on all tests. His efforts paid off by preparing him to make maximum scores on many of his training and physical tests. He received a written commendation for achieving a perfect score of 400 points on the physical proficiency testing. With the completion of his advanced infantry

15

training at Fort Jackson, South Carolina, Ross becoming a well-trained and sharply honed fighting man. For the first time in his life, however, he recognized for sure that he was not ten feet tall and that he definitely was not bulletproof. This realization was a positive step for him as he began to face the harsh realities of life and the fact that there were enemies in the world who were out to get him and who would jump at the chance to take his life. He knew that in the very near future, he would be thrust into the reality of such a situation. He wondered if indeed he was properly prepared to meet the challenge of confronting the enemy on the enemy's home turf. The next stops for Jerry were California and eventually Vietnam. Moreover, in spite of his brashness, he knew that he was not in the right place, spiritually speaking.

Upon arriving in California, Jerry was assigned to a replacement unit and given final preparations for shipment to Vietnam. He and his contemporaries were assembled for transfer to the Vietnamese theatre of war from the base in California. The United States Air Force supplied the transportation in the form of a cargo plane. The accommodations of the plane were very primitive and without the normal comforts that were apparent in civilian airliners. The troops had to sit on very poor seats while facing the back of the plane during flight. The whole arrangement was very spartan and totally without regard for the comfort of the troops. Flying backward was definitely uncomfortable for Jerry Ross. He became nauseated early in the flight and suffered the consequences of airsickness for the entire flight. He arrived in Vietnam in a weakened condition because of the airsickness. Jerry entered this period of his life in a spiritually sick condition. Knowing that he would possibly meet death head on in encounters with the enemy, the realization that he was not right with God, the Heavenly Father, began to weigh heavier and heavier on Jerry's inner being.

Although he felt he was properly trained and prepared as a soldier for the situation he was facing, Jerry was sadly lacking in the most important aspect of his life. After all the years of saying no to God's overtures and knocking, he continued to disregard the testimonies of Christian witnesses and to push God aside. Even while he was facing the most serious ordeal and challenge of his life, Jerry neglected the most important preparation of all. He continued to reject the possibility of a healthy and fulfilling spiritual life promised by a loving and patient Heavenly Father in return for Jerry's confession of his sins and acceptance of Jesus Christ into his heart. Jerry Ross now fully realized the gravity of his rejection of God at that time, but he was very thankful that a patient and loving God kept dealing with him and extending his marvelous Grace despite Jerry's apparent disregard of the Spirit's persistent pleading.

Upon his arrival in Vietnam, Jerry and his fellow soldiers were carried to a building that reminded him of a chicken house back home in Alabama with its curtains down. He and his friends discovered right away that this primitive building would be their home for the near future. The building did have a concrete floor but very little other convenience. While the soldiers were still settling into their new quarters, a member of the cadre came in, and with a very loud voice, began to prepare them for their first night on foreign soil. This made the new soldiers wonder if all their superiors yelled all the time when dealing with new soldiers. They had heard the yelling since the beginning of basic training.

The non-commissioned officer warned the new soldiers that their compound would most likely come under a mortar attack that first night. Further traumatizing these young men who were fresh from the United States, the non-com stated that people could be killed that very night in that very area. Additionally, he stated that they should cover themselves with mattresses in an effort to avoid or minimize the effect of the shrapnel. He really got their attention when he said, "If you can't find a mattress for cover, cover yourselves with the body of another dead soldier. That will protect you." That grisly advice from the cadre man served as a macabre reminder of what was ahead. The young soldiers' fear was compounded by the actions of the artillery batteries on the base that kept firing 105-mm howitzer artillery pieces the entire night. Once the howitzer shells were fired, they generated a sound that resembled the sound of a mortar round coming in. Thinking that they were being mortared, Jerry and his fellow soldiers were on edge the entire time. Sleep or rest was entirely out of the question that night. Fortunately, there were no enemy hits on Jerry's compound that sleepless night. He and his soldier friends remained at that compound for three days while awaiting transfer to their assigned home bases.

After the three days had passed, Jerry was transferred to Vietnam's Vinh Long base by helicopter for assignment to the military unit that was to be his home base. Upon his arrival there, he was assigned to a cabin

17

(commonly called a "hootch") that was to be his home for an undetermined time. As an infantryman with advanced training, Ross was initially assigned to duty as a guard at a perimeter outpost. Up to that time, there had been no army infantrymen on the base, but a platoon was being established for the purpose of guarding the Vinh Long helicopter base.

The Vinh Long Base was home to the largest aviation battalion in Vietnam at the time, and one of considerable importance because of its mission. The battalion stationed at Vinh Long operated several types of helicopters and used them around the clock as they provided transportation service to field units of the American forces and, at times, as they provided the same services to the South Vietnamese military units. Helicopter warfare was a fairly new concept at that time and one that was being developed in the Vietnam conflict. Experienced helicopter pilots such as Colonel Jack Dempsey and other field officers felt that the use of helicopters could be a very valuable tool in the rapid deployment of troops to areas where new engagements of the enemy were taking place. They also felt that the ability to move troops and supplies quickly to the scene of new battles was an important advantage. An additional advantage of the use of helicopters in actual battle operations was the ability to quickly withdraw troops from untenable situations and positions. Also, by arming the helicopters, army leaders felt that they could transform the lowly helicopter into a formidable fighting machine.

Whether ferrying troops, supplies, or ordnance, the courageous crews many times flew directly into the face of the enemy troops and fire as they performed their missions. When their missions were completed, the crews flew back to the home base to rest or to pick up new assignments. Any crew could be called upon to fly several missions during a day. The important thing was that they be protected while they were on the ground at their home base and vulnerable to mortar fire. Initially, Specialist Ross and his counterparts were assigned to that duty.

Shortly after arriving in Vietnam and being assigned to a home base, Jerry was the victim of a freakish off-duty happening. He and some of his friends had gone into a small town near the base late one day to relax and have a few drinks. While there, they saw a young boy standing on the street with several brightly colored balloons. He handed one to Jerry and it exploded in Jerry's face as he took it. It turned out that the balloons were filled with hydrogen. Jerry received some severe burns about the face and

18

head that required hospitalization for treatment. He returned to his unit and was on light duty for several days.

The home base was in a vulnerable location, and as such, was a favorite target of the Viet Cong forces. A large number of helicopters would be on the ground at any given time while being serviced or reloaded for runs to the battle zones. Although the Viet Cong would attack at any time, their forte was stealthy nighttime hit-and-run operations. Defending the Vinh Long base against such attacks was the mission of Jerry Ross and the other infantry soldiers in the newly formed battalion. In addition to providing base protection, Jerry and his group were helping in an operation to train South Vietnamese soldiers (ARVN) in certain aspects of helicopter warfare, namely, the speedy helicopter transportation of troops and ordnance to different zones of operations. Delivery of troops and equipment to the battle zone by helicopter was a new tactic and one that demonstrated great promise, but the unloading procedures in the battle zone had to be done very fast and efficiently. As a result of that important requirement, United States military officials believed that the South Vietnamese troops, as allies, needed to be trained in the basics of helicopter warfare.

Once again, fate knocked on Jerry Ross's door and his world was about to change again at whirlwind speed. Upon reviewing his weapons training scores from Fort Jackson and other information, the officers asked Jerry to be a door gunner on a helicopter. He had demonstrated his skills with machine guns as well as other weapons. Unbelievably, within a short time after arriving in Vietnam, Jerry was flying missions as a door gunner on a transport helicopter. A door gunner must have all the weapons skills in order to successfully defend his ship during the heat of battle and during pickups and deliveries in combat zones. In Jerry's mind at the time, he felt that flying was much better than walking, and he jumped at the chance to be a door gunner. Little did he know what his new job would become and the dangers it would produce. At this particular time, he had pushed the Spirit of God into the background of his mind and it was not pursuing him as vigorously as in some past times. The Spirit was still at work, albeit more quietly, in placing Jerry in the proper place for the big test that was coming in his future.

Soon after his arrival in Vietnam and before he began duty as a door gunner, Jerry was on duty in the area of his compound when the base came under a fierce mortar attack by the Viet Cong. He was outside the huts

19

at the time and was hit by shrapnel when a mortar round exploded near him. The wound earned him the Purple Heart. This was his first medal earned in combat.

The new assignment as a door gunner was a welcome change in the beginning. The early flights for Jerry were mainly for ferrying supplies and troops to outpost areas and, as such, were not engaging the enemy forces in combat. Many times, the gunners would be allowed to get some target practice in free-fire zones on the return trips to the base. They mainly shot trees and other objects on the ground, anything to sharpen their skills. During this period, Jerry set a personal goal to do his best and to learn how to be a good door gunner. He was driven to be the best door gunner in the group. Through those exercises and personal determination, Jerry became a highly skilled door gunner on the supply helicopters (commonly known as "slicks" in the soldiers' vernacular). One of the skills he developed was the ability to direct his fire underneath the airborne chopper and to the front and rear of the helicopter while the unit was in flight. This particular skill served Jerry and his crewmates well on a number of occasions and added an extra dimension to the art of protecting a helicopter in flight. The pilot knew that if he had a skilled gunner directing heavy fire to the sides of and underneath the slick, he could maneuver to safety with a greater chance of success. Jerry knew that as long as the unit was in flight, he had a degree of safety and that he was still alive. In view of his spiritually lost condition at the time, he had a great fear of dying because he knew what his destiny would be in eternity.

During the short time he was flying as a door gunner on the slicks, Jerry and his unit were airlifting reinforcements and supplies into a combat zone over a seven-hour period of time. Following that action, Jerry's ship and crew were returning to the battle zone once again to pick up crash survivors and battle-weary South Vietnamese troops. Six helicopter transports were shot down in the heavy fighting that occurred on February 15, 1967. Their crews and the South Vietnamese soldiers (ARVN) that were being rotated out of the action were still on the ground and in the fight of their lives against the hardcore North Vietnamese troops. The South Vietnamese defenders were pinned down and were on the very brink of being overrun by the aggressor forces. Death was a distinct possibility for them.

After several trips of transporting replacement soldiers and supplies to the battle zone, the transport ships were bringing war-weary troops back to bases behind the battle lines. During that time, Jerry Ross distinguished himself during three particularly dangerous extraction missions. The pilot of his ship stated that as soon as the helicopter had landed in the pickup zone on the first extraction mission, Ross immediately jumped from it and ran at least twenty-five meters through sniper fire and sporadic mortar action to the weary soldiers. He then began to get them organized to get on board the chopper the quickest possible way. Through the whistling bullets, he urged the soldiers to get moving. During this time, he physically carried one soldier all the way to the ship while urging the others to get on the helicopter as quickly as possible. Ross's ship was able to depart the area and carry the exhausted fighters to a safe mobilization area.

Minutes later, his ship returned to the battle zone a second time and landed again to pick up more of the South Vietnamese soldiers. During this second mission, the pilot observed Specialist Ross leap from the ship into enemy fire, so that he could expedite the loading operation while helping the troops aboard. Without regard to his personal safety, he carried some of the wounded Vietnamese fighting men from their field positions to his ship while directing the others to the ship. Once again, the helicopter was able to leave the battle zone and fly the troops to safety. The pilot continued his statement of Jerry's heroic actions by saying that the determined efforts of Jerry Ross greatly reduced the ship's time on the ground and allowed it to accomplish its mission. Jerry Ross and his ship returned to the scorched and burning landing area yet a third time, where Ross, once again and without regard for his own safety, repeated his heroic actions in the same manner as before. His actions were dauntless as he moved to help the last of the Vietnamese aboard the ship. He lifted them on swiftly and made several trips into the battle zone to carry their heavy loads, thereby loading the helicopter in record time. The pilot of Jerry's ship said, "Specialist Ross's gallant actions under fire saved the Vietnamese from further injury and denied the Viet Cong the opportunity to inflict damage to our flight. I feel his courageous efforts in those critical moments contributed enormously to the successful completion of the mission."

Another officer said the following of Jerry's heroic actions: "His aggressive actions at this time saved many Vietnamese lives and prevented needless damage to his ship and casualties to his crew. His courage and boldness are in keeping with the highest traditions of the military service and reflect great credit upon himself and the United States Army."

As a result of his exemplary gallantry during that operation, Jerry Ross was awarded the Army Commendation Medal with "V" device for his heroism and unflinching service to his county and his fellow soldiers. He also received his official Purple Heart for wounds received in an earlier operation. The awards were presented by General William Westmoreland.

Jerry Ross did not view his actions in that operation as heroic. He says that his concern at the time was to stay alive. His goal in that mission was to get the South Vietnamese troops aboard the transport as fast as he could and get out of the zone as quickly as possible. If the quickest way to get a war-weary and wounded soldier aboard was to carry him aboard, Jerry Ross was more than willing to do that. Although he performed unquestionably heroic deeds at that time, he had the ulterior motive of self-preservation. Recalling his mother's teaching, he knew that he was an unsaved person at the time and that he would not go to heaven if he died in that condition.

Word of Jerry's skill as a door gunner circulated around the Vinh Long base; in a very short time, he was chosen to be a gunner on a helicopter gunship. Gunships were specially equipped units that carried a large amount of ordnance used in air-to-ground warfare. Personnel assigned to duty on those ships were exposed to extreme danger because of the close contact with the enemy and his weapons. Gunships were awesome fighting machines due to their weaponry and the highly trained crews operating them. Whereas helicopters were used primarily for transportation of troops and supplies in earlier conflicts such as the Korean War, the Vietnam War was becoming a fertile ground for the development of the helicopter as a fighting machine. In the beginning, conventional helicopters were modified by the addition of weaponry (primarily large-caliber machine guns) in order to provide them with the capability of attacking the enemy while assisting friendly troops on the ground. Helicopter warfare has continued to evolve positively in equipment and techniques even until the present day, thereby making present-day helicopters formidable opponents for the enemy. Lessons learned in the Vietnam War provided a solid experience base for the development techniques and equipment used today.

In an effort to gain an additional edge on the enemy during the Vietnamese conflict, the gunship unit had one helicopter that was rigged to lay smoke screens. Vast amounts of smoke could be generated very simply by injecting a heavy oil into the exhaust of the jet engine that powered the helicopter. The exhaust gases from the helicopter's engine were extremely hot, which made it very easy to generate large volumes of dense smoke. That helicopter (affectionately known as "Ole Smoky") was a vital part of engaging the enemy troops. It was often called on to lay a smoke screen between American troops and the enemy. The smoke was so intense that the American troops would have time to take up new tactical positions before the smoke cleared. American forces learned later that the North Vietnamese troops thought the smoke from "Ole Smoky" contained noxious chemicals. Thinking this, the enemy troops would fall flat on the ground or seek other cover, thereby allowing the U.S. troops the time needed to re-deploy to more strategic positions. During his tour of duty, Jerry was an eyewitness to the use and value of "Ole Smoky."

Once assigned to the gunship unit, Ross began to fly combat missions on a regular basis. Although the missions were far from routine in many cases, they were all dangerous. The stress of those multiple daily missions would build up on Jerry and his crewmates, forcing them to find ways of preparing themselves mentally for the job at hand. He and his crewmates would return to the base in the evenings after flying missions and attempt to relax and unwind. Sadly, they would choose the wrong way to do that. The Enlisted Men's Club offered a worldly solution to their problems: drinking. Drinking had a way of making them forget the myriad of challenges the faced on a given day. They would drink alcoholic beverages until very late in the night (or the wee hours of the morning). In those almost-daily skirmishes with the enemy, he often thought that his luck might run out at any time. He knew that he was not prepared for that possibility because he had not made peace with God. In some of those times, he would promise God that he would do better if He would bring him out of the present danger. Then, at the end of the day's missions, when he was safely back at the home base, it was back to the bottle for him. Sometimes Jerry and his friends would dress in civilian clothes and go into the nearest village to unwind. Occasionally they would incite fights in the bars and on the streets of the village. On those occasions, promises Jerry made to God earlier in the day were broken in a very few hours as he resorted to the ill-gotten and misleading comfort offered by alcohol. Today he wonders many times why God continued to be merciful to him when he was being totally obstinate and insubordinate toward the Heavenly Father. He knows fully now and testifies that it was only through grace!

Specialist Ross continued his assignment as a door gunner on the slicks for a short period of time. During that time, he was improving his skills and building a reputation as a gunner. A skillful, observant, and resourceful door gunner was an absolutely essential member of any helicopter fighting team. As his skills and ability as a door gunner got better and better, he caught the eye of the Colonel Jack T. Dempsey, commander of the Thirteenth Combat Aviation Battalion, the group that flew the assault helicopters. Upon being asked if he would accept transfer to that group and be Colonel Dempsey's door gunner, Jerry volunteered. He accepted the assignment and moved directly to Colonel Dempsey's unit. It was an honor, indeed, to be recognized and asked to be the door gunner on the commander's ship, especially to be asked by the colonel himself. Thus began the most memorable and dangerous time in Jerry Ross's service in the U.S. Army.

Colonel Jack Dempsey was a soldier's soldier and one who had a great rapport with the members of his battalion, especially the enlisted men. Colonel Dempsey was an older man and much like a father figure to those young men serving under him. This did not mean that he was a soft touch by any stretch of the imagination. He respected his subordinates as important members of the organization and they respected him because of his character and outstanding demeanor. He was a commander who would not ask his men to do anything he would not do. He had served in the last months of World War II and in the Korean War, and had an exemplary record as a soldier in those conflicts. He was awarded the Silver Star, two Purple Hearts, and a cluster of other medals in those wars. Another army pilot said, "He was one great leader. You just knew that he wouldn't be sitting behind his desk. He was always out where the action was." Colonel Dempsey had a deep concern for his men and would go to great lengths to be with them when they were involved in skirmishes with the enemy.

24

As a respected commander, he was always ready to share the lessons of his many wartime experiences for the benefit of his troops.

As Jerry Ross joined the Thirteenth Combat Aviation Battalion, he was stepping into a different type of service. The Thirteenth Group—also known as the famed Delta Battalion—had the responsibility of flying dangerous helicopter assault missions for the three South Vietnamese army divisions in the IV Corps Area. They also ferried supplies and troops for the South Vietnamese army groups as a part of their mission.

Another responsibility assigned to Colonel Dempsey was that of flying visiting dignitaries, high-ranking United States military officers, and the news media personnel over the area and to various outposts near the active combat zones. Jerry Ross and the other members of Colonel Dempsey's personal crew enjoyed these sorties, during which they would be allowed to rub shoulders with generals and other dignitaries. Rather than delegating this responsibility, Colonel Dempsey and his crew chose to perform this duty themselves for a number of reasons. By doing the task themselves, they could control the objective of the missions and provide a safer atmosphere for their passengers.

Colonel Dempsey and his crew also flew combat-rated missions during that time. Jerry Ross was the door gunner on all of these missions. They supported the South Vietnamese troops to the greatest extent possible, facing danger all the while. A couple of months went by as Colonel Dempsey and his crew continued to fly those missions in support of the South Vietnamese army troops as they engaged the North Vietnamese troops and Viet Cong in skirmishes on the ground. In many cases, these battles resulted in fierce and close-range combat, with heavy casualties on both sides. It was during one of these battles that Colonel Dempsey was mortally wounded. Specialist Jerry Ross once again distinguished himself with yet another display of uncommon valor and exceptional heroism and gallantry.

On Easter Sunday, March 26, 1967, Battalion Commander Dempsey and his crew, including Specialist Ross as door gunner, were flying as observers of an air mobile operation against the North Vietnamese being conducted about eighteen miles southwest on the Vinh Long base. Since the operation was not going as well as planned, a decision was made to do a tactical withdrawal of the South Vietnamese troops who were spearheading the thrust into enemy territory. During the first lift of South

Vietnamese forces from the battle area by other helicopters of the Thirteenth Combat Aviation Battalion, the transport helicopters came under intense enemy fire coming from the well-fortified bunkers and other gun emplacements surrounding the landing area. As the helicopters departed, one was disabled and unable to leave the area. A second helicopter was shot down while trying to rescue the crew of the first one. The situation was getting worse by the minute and was fast becoming untenable as an offensive operation.

Colonel Dempsey and his crew were observing the action as they hovered and circled their command helicopter a safe distance away from the actual fighting. Seeing the alarming turn of events, Dempsey knew that something had to be done immediately if his downed crews were to be saved. Calling on the lessons of previous experiences, he made an immediate decision to go into the landing zone in an effort to rescue the crews from very severe danger. Knowing the dangers that his crew would be facing in the rescue attempt and that a number of the downed crews were wounded, Colonel Dempsey asked Specialist Ross and the other crewmen if they would volunteer to fly the mission. Specialist Ross immediately volunteered to fly in, leave the ship, and help the wounded soldiers and others into his ship. Having done a similar task in a similar situation at an earlier date, Ross knew well the dangers he would face when on the ground, particularly since he did not have a good knowledge of the status of the crews already downed in the landing zone. Without regard and concern for his own safety and with full knowledge of the very present danger to his life, Jerry Ross volunteered for the mission without hesitation. In an attempt to soften up the resistance of the enemy troops, Colonel Dempsey and the crew called in and coordinated air strikes on the enemy just before beginning their descent into the landing zone.

As Colonel Dempsey began his descent toward the landing zone, his helicopter came into the range of enemy fire. The helicopter took a number of bullet hits from sporadic fire during the approach. As it neared the ground, the gunfire became much more intense. When the helicopter was within about five feet of touchdown, the enemy directed extremely intense machine gun fire into the cockpit area from the right side of the aircraft. The pilot, Colonel Dempsey, took a fatal hit to his head during that particularly intense fusillade of enemy fire. The co-pilot took over the controls and landed the ship in what amounted to a crash landing.

Seeing that his commander had been hit, Specialist Jerry Ross immediately went forward to check on him, braving a hail of enemy machine gun bullets coming from the right side of the craft. The bullets continued to strike Colonel Dempsey. Jerry noted that the co-pilot had been wounded twice and he immediately pushed him from the aircraft. Upon checking the condition of his commander, Jerry discovered that he was dead as a result of an enemy bullet wound to the head. After that determination, Specialist Ross once again shoved the wounded co-pilot, Major Casper, from the craft and then jumped from the helicopter himself and informed the crew chief that the craft was no longer flyable. Ross then stepped forward and began to help remove a wounded soldier who had been previously loaded onto the helicopter.

Following this, Jerry crawled alongside a dike while encouraging the troops and crews from the downed helicopters who were pinned down in the landing zone. He otherwise inspired them to take any available cover and keep fighting. He then secured a radio and informed the mission commander of the status of the battalion commander and the other wounded troops. At first, the gunship pilots hovering and circling the area were reluctant to follow the directions of Ross because they didn't recognize the voice coming over the radio. After he had established his identity as Colonel Dempsey's door gunner, Ross then directed gunship strikes and jet fighter plane strafing and bombing on the Viet Cong troops he was observing. He continued to do so until the radio ceased to operate. He remained calm and in control during the four-hour ordeal, even though there was an imminent danger of his position being overrun by the Viet Cong forces. Jerry stood in complete amazement at the firepower the Viet Cong troops could bring to bear on the trapped Allied forces. Without the aid of vehicles of any type, the Viet Cong were able to bring the necessary weaponry to the battle front on their backs as they traversed the narrow trails of the woodlands and swamps. Sometimes when navigable water was available, they would transport their weapons by sampans or other homemade boats. It seemed that the enemy forces solved very difficult logistics problems by physical strength, numbers of troops, determination, and stealth.

During the time of the fierce offensive maneuver by the Viet Cong during their attack, Jerry came into a full realization that his life was hanging by a thread and that it could be ended at any moment. For the first time, he did some serious praying and called upon God for deliverance. He made some serious promises to Him and said that he would make the required changes in his life if he could be spared. At the time, Jerry then felt a twinge of inner peace, felt there might be a chance that he and the other troops could be rescued. That trying time proved to be the beginning of the decline of his strong "I don't need anybody" attitude. Specialist Jerry Ross finally realized fully that there is a God and that he needed God in his life. He says this day that he knows that God can and will hear the prayer of a sinner if the prayer is offered in sincerity. To this day, Jerry doesn't know why he didn't ask God to save him. He says that he didn't really know how to seek God's plan of salvation at the time he was in Vietnam.

During the four hours following the crash of Colonel Dempsey's helicopter and two others also downed by enemy fire, the crews from the downed helicopters were pinned down by extremely heavy enemy fire. They were fortunate to have a low dike between them and the Viet Cong forces; this provided a small measure of protection from the blistering fire. The helicopter commanders hovering around the engagement area called in air strikes by jet fighters and additional helicopter gunships. The jet fighters came from more than one base and every available gunship in the area was called in to drive the Viet Cong back in a well-coordinated counterattack. Those units delivered intense fire to the enemy during the offensive. The air force jets, in addition to heavy strafing of the Viet Cong, bombed the enemy as a part of the engagement.

Near the end of the counterattack, Ole Smoky (the smoke-generating helicopter) was called in to lay a heavy smokescreen between the pinned-down Allied forces and the enemy. With the thick smokescreen in place, transport helicopters and others were able to land and recover the Allied troops, albeit with considerable difficulty. The unit that picked up Jerry Ross was greatly overloaded and experienced extreme difficulty in becoming airborne, but was able to do so after several attempts due to the remarkable skill of the pilot. The troops, including the wounded, were safely airlifted back to the home base. Thus ended field events of the eventful Easter Sunday of March 26, 1967.

The return to the home base late in the day on that Easter Sunday was a poignant time for Specialist Jerry Ross. As the rescue helicopters approached the landing zone with their weary and worn human cargo,

Jerry beheld a scene that that warmed his heart. It was a scene of many activities and of dedicated cooperation as the base personnel, cooks, medics, enlisted men, and officers each worked feverishly to refuel and arm the helicopters for return trips to the battle zone. Quick meals were given to the crews as their ships were refitted for further action. Those persons who were fortunate enough to remain on the base that day were hastily working together completing the jobs that needed to be done without regard to their MOS (the military term for their job descriptions). Officers and enlisted men were working side by side, oblivious to the status and privileges of rank. Jerry Ross was impressed and touched by the concern of the base personnel, as they unselfishly did the things necessary to support their comrades who were fighting in the field. Such camaraderie among fighting men is quite common, but is a characteristic that is often overlooked by the news media and others. There is a strong brotherhood of service men fighting for a common cause. The outstanding work by all the personnel at the home air base continued until all casualties, alive and dead, were recovered along with the South Vietnamese troops. In retrospect, Jerry realized that all the people who were supporting the operation from the home base with such vigor and unselfishness were doing it in full support of their military brothers who were fighting on the front lines. Looking back to that specific situation, Jerry said that he is reminded of the sacrifice that Jesus made for him. He also says that God protected him when he was in terrific danger. Jerry was seeking protection from the flying bullets at that time, but God's grace was applied in great measure; Jerry found mercy when he was in deep trouble, physically and spiritually. To his regret, he failed to keep the promises he made that day.

The events of Easter Sunday in 1967 were earthshaking to Jerry; he suddenly began to realize that he was mortal and that any one of the hundreds, perhaps thousands of bullets that sprayed around him that day could have ended his life. He saw his commander, Colonel Jack Dempsey, get killed in action that day and others of his crew receive severe wounds during the same battlefield action. During the heat of battle, Jerry had called upon God and promised Him that if He would spare him and get him out of the present situation alive, he would accept Him and serve Him. During that special time, he felt the presence and call of God in a way he had never felt Him before. Thus began the decline of Jerry's lackadaisical attitude toward God and the growth of a realization—for perhaps the first time—that he needed God in his life. The gravity of the situation got his attention at the time of the fierce battle, and it seemed that God had finally gained a toehold in his life, at least momentarily. It seemed at the time that Jerry had developed a degree of sincerity toward God in his life and was ready to repent and seek forgiveness for the multitude of sins of his past life. He was at the very point of accepting Christ as his Savior. That was not to be, however, as Jerry returned to his old ways shortly after arriving back at the home base, thereby thwarting God's plan for his life once again.

After safely returning to base completely untouched by all the enemy fire whistling by him during the day's battle, Jerry quickly fell back into his customary routine that usually followed his day's work as a door gunner. That routine consisted of meeting his friends at the base Enlisted Men's (NCO) Club and drinking various alcoholic beverages till the wee hours of morning. On that particular day, Easter Sunday of 1967, the group of friends gathered at the NCO Club for the usual round of conversation and lots of drinks. As the effect of the alcohol clouded Jerry's mind, the Prince of Darkness intervened and Jerry Ross completely faltered in keeping the promises he had made to his Creator just a few hours before. Outwardly, he knowingly and by choice put forth the image of a macho man while the forces of good and evil were at war in his inner being. The battle going on there was far more important that the battle he had been through earlier that day.

If the forces of evil triumphed and were chosen by Jerry, the ultimate victor in the battle was hell. Jerry Ross now realizes that, once again, God in his infinite patience was not giving up on him and that it was *only through grace* that he survived the army years.

The remarkable courage, exceptional valor, and complete disregard for his own safety exhibited by Specialist Jerry Ross during the heat of battle on March 27, 1967 were observed by a number of officers and enlisted men. Their documentation of the event and recommendation for a suitable decoration recognizing Specialist Ross's heroism and gallant actions were submitted to higher command echelons for consideration. Originally, Jerry was being recommended to receive the Bronze Star Decoration in recognition of his heroic actions that Easter. When the recommendation papers were presented to the high-level Review Board for its approval, the board recommended a higher award. As a result of the recommendation, the board and the president of the United States authorized the award of the Silver Star to Specialist Jerry E. Ross for his gallantry in action. The Certificate of Award, dated May 27, 1967, and the Silver Star Medal were presented to Specialist Ross by General William Westmoreland, Commander of United States Military Forces in the Republic of South Vietnam.

The happenings of March 27, 1967 had a profound effect on Specialist Jerry Ross. The images of his commander's death while trying to save his trapped comrades were especially traumatic. To lose a respected and highly decorated leader and friend so quickly proved to be an especially trying time for Ross. Making the situation even more heartbreaking was the fact that Colonel Dempsey, a married father of four children, was approved for promotion to the rank of brigadier general at the time of his death. At a later date, Jerry had to stand before General Westmoreland and give the details surrounding the death of Colonel Jack Dempsey. Seeing Major Casper, the co-pilot, and other comrades wounded in the battle merely added to the sorrow Jerry felt at the time. All of these happenings and activities brought about some noticeable changes, both inwardly and outwardly, in Jerry Ross's life. He learned that he was mortal and that he needed God in his life. Another lesson that he learned was that the "tough guy" image he had been exhibiting for years was wrong.

Shortly after the events on and associated with the March 27, 1067 operation, Jerry returned to his old home base at Vinh Long. He had extended his tour of duty in Vietnam by forty-five days and had just begun the extension on that Easter Sunday. He decided to recall the extension and return to the States. He flew very few missions after he returned to his old base. The changes wrought in his attitude and life by the Easter Sunday actions robbed him of his desire and ability to meet the enemy head on and challenge him on his home turf. He no longer had the heart to do the daring things as a door gunner that had been commonplace for him on previous missions. The skills were still there but the will was not there.

Winning the Silver Star had a more profound impact on Jerry's comrades in arms than it did on him. They more or less placed him on a pedestal and accorded him the deserved status of hero. They were in awe of his valor and actions beyond the call of duty on that Easter Sunday, March 27, 1967. Jerry was later interviewed by reporters from the Los Angeles Times and Look magazine regarding the overall operation, Colonel Dempsey's untimely death, and Jerry's assessment of the complete operation. Jerry, however, definitely did not see himself as a hero or as doing anything extraordinary at the time. He says that he was just trying to stay alive and was helping his fellow soldiers do the same. Jerry gave God the credit for his actions on that day and for bringing him through the perils of battle, and he still gives Him complete credit for it all till the present day. Like many other medal winners, Jerry Ross has been extremely quiet about his part in the action that earned him the Silver Star. After being decorated for valor, he chose to talk very little, if at all, about it and has continued that practice till the present. In fact, a number of his friends know little to nothing about his army service. For several reasons, he refrained from talking about his army exploits, for fear of being perceived as a braggart by those about him. He was concerned about discussing the issue, fearing that he might begin to take credit for his actions and leave God out of the picture. He could not shake the guilt and remorse he felt because he had broken his promises to God.

The remainder of Jerry Ross's time in Vietnam was basically uneventful. Orders for his transfer back to the United States came down from headquarters. Jerry was discharged from the United States Armed Forces upon his arrival in California. He was once again a civilian with a veteran's memories of twenty-one months of his life that were packed with hard work, battles, danger, tragedy, and some wild times. Perhaps the most troubling memory was the memory of broken promises to God and the fact that he had trampled God's grace under his feet after he survived an extremely dangerous battle during those twenty-one months. A new phase of his life was about to begin, but he was still a lost person, spiritually speaking. God was still patiently calling and extending His marvelous grace.

Specialist 4 Jerry Ross completed his tour of duty in the Vietnam conflict and received his orders to be transferred back to the United States. He arrived at a California military base without further incident and prepared to be discharged. Upon completing all the requirements for discharge from the armed services and placement into the Army Reserve program, Jerry Ross was officially discharged from the United States Army on June 26, 1967. With his military obligation fulfilled, he returned to his Alabama home near Boaz to enter the next phase of his life.

Private Jerry Ross as a recruit

Picture of sign near the main entrance to Fort Gordon, Georgia taken by Jerry Ross shortly after his arrival there.

Helicopters in formation over Mekong Delta. Picture taken by Jerry Ross.

Helicopters on a mission. Note smoke from bomb dropped on forest. This is one of Jerry's favorite pictures.

A helicopter flying in formation with Jerry Ross's unit. The view is from the door gunner's position.

Jerry's photograph of a typical street

Jerry and friends during off duty hours

Specialists Jerry Ross's Bronze Star medal

Specialist Jerry Ross's Silver Star medal. The award of the Silver Star was presented to Jerry by General William Westmoreland. The award certificate was signed by General Westmoreland.

The Cross of Gallantry, the highest decoration awarded by the government of South Vietnam

The Army Commendation Medal

Jerry Ross's Purple Heart Medal

The Air Medal awarded to recognize a minimum of 55 hours in aerial combat by a member of the United States Armed Forces.

Photograph of Specialist Jerry Ross with medals displayed around the photograph. The Silver Star Decoration is the top left decoration. Going clockwise from that point, the decorations are as follows: Bronze Star, Vietnamese Cross of Gallantry, Army Commendation Medal with V device, Purple Heart, Air Medal, Vietnamese Campaign Medal, Combat Infantryman's Badge, Republic of Vietnam Service Medal, National Defense Medal. Jerry's original collar brass and dog tag can be seen at the top of the picture.

CHAPTER 3

THE POST-WAR YEARS AFTER VIETNAM

Returning home from Vietnam was a time of mixed emotions for Jerry Ross. On the one hand, he was extremely relieved that he had survived the dangers he had faced in the war zone. On the other hand, however, there was the remorse he felt because of the broken promises made to the Almighty during the heat of battle. It seemed to him that every heartbeat was a solemn reminder that he had failed God on a tremendous scale. It was as if God was saying, "You committed to Me that you would change your life if I would bring you out of Vietnam. I have kept My promise. What about you?" Those same heartbeats also signified to Jerry an additional segment of life that God extended to him through another application of His marvelous and matchless grace. The haunting broken promises were a constant heavy weight on his inner being, a weight that seemed to get heavier each day he carried it.

Although being back home was a welcome change for Jerry, it meant that he was going to have to change his lifestyle if he was to fit into the day-to-day relationships he was likely to encounter in his northeast Alabama home. The gung-ho, hard-drinking, hard-fighting, and rowdy life he had lived prior to military service and in Vietnam would never be accepted by

43

his family and friends. Sadly, Jerry Ross was not prepared to give up that lifestyle, and as a result, was destined to face society as a "misfit."

Upon returning home, Jerry lived with his parents for several months. Although they were thankful and happy to have him back home, they could not accept the way he was living. They were happy to provide a home for him, but it had to be by their rules. For example, his father would not allow him to bring any alcoholic beverages into the house. Further, if Mr. Ross happened to find beer in Jerry's car, he would pour it out. Hermus and Ruby Ross, being loving parents, talked to their son about the error of his ways and the great need for him to get his "house in order." His parents expected him to live the way they were living as Christians and to avoid the very thought of drinking, wild parties, fighting, and staying out all night. They wanted him to be in church where, hopefully, he would hear the Good News of the Gospel, be convicted of his sins, and accept God. They felt strongly that the association with God's people would have a positive effect on Jerry and would eventually break his desire to run from God and to continue to reject Him.

Jerry initially tried to abide by the rules laid down by his parents, but his extreme need to "drown his troubles" soon won the battle. The raging battle going on within him, when coupled with his external demeanor and almost insatiable desire for some kind of peace to come into his life, created an extremely critical situation. Because of his self-created and -proclaimed "macho" image, Jerry was fighting the battle by himself, not realizing that divine help was available for the asking. He desperately longed for just one day of peace and escape from his troubled state, but he could never seem to find it. Jerry resorted to attending parties and other outings sponsored by his friends in quest of that peace. Alcohol was almost always present at those functions, as were some of the drugs of the culture, namely speed. None of that activity fulfilled his inner needs, and many times he would slip away from the parties and go to sleep. Tragically, he failed to see that resorting to alcohol and drugs was not the way to find that peace and escape he so desperately desired. Although Jerry was beginning to entertain thoughts of getting his life in order at that time, he was still unwilling to accept the overtures of the Holy Spirit as it moved to convict him. He felt he could get his life in order by doing things his own way.

During that time, Jerry began working locally at the Guntersville Spinning Mill, known colloquially as the Cotton Mill. He had applied for unemployment benefits shortly after returning home from Vietnam, but, ironically, he finally got the job with the Cotton Mill on the day his unemployment benefits were to begin. Working at the mill was mild and uneventful employment, indeed, when compared to serving as a door gunner for a helicopter gunship. Working in the Cotton Mill was also a welcome change from the terrible stress and anxiety experienced during the dangerous months he served in the battle zone in Vietnam. Even while employed at the Cotton Mill, Jerry continued the partying, replete with drinking. At first, he was marginally able to satisfy the requirements of the job, even though he worked a number of shifts while experiencing the full effect of an acute hangover. As time went by, his chosen lifestyle began to tell on him and he eventually lost his job with the mill.

A number of family clashes occurred because of the difference between the Rosses' Christian rules and Jerry's chosen lifestyle. His parents wanted him to get his life in order and live the Christian life he had heard about since his youthful years. They knew about some of his problems, but he was able to hide a number of the more debilitating ones from them. Unwilling to accept and live by his parents' rules, he soon made a decision to move out of the Ross home and go to Toledo, Ohio in search of work. Jerry did not want his chosen lifestyle to be cramped by his parents' demands.

During that critical time of his life, Jerry Ross found that the inner peace he was seeking so desperately was indeed a very elusive commodity. That was in addition to the fact that he was still suffering turmoil inwardly because of the promises that he had made to God back in Vietnam and then had broken immediately. To add even more to the load his conscience was carrying at the time, the Holy Spirit was applying His convicting power to Jerry Ross in full measure. Jerry said of the situation, "When a man gets under conviction and says he is not lost and doesn't know the difference, then he is not under the convicting power of God that I was under." Jerry was definitely experiencing true conviction in his heart because of the sinful life he was living, but he was still not ready to make the needed change. He was still trampling God's grace under his feet.

While all those familial differences were taking place in addition to the constant presence of the Holy Spirit's convicting power, Jerry Ross was still masquerading as a tough guy with a willingness to party or fight at the drop of a hat. Inwardly, however, he was deeply troubled about his sinful way of living, but he was unwilling to do anything about it. The inward conflict had a full-time presence in his life and was fast becoming a load he was unable to bear, but thankfully, the Grace of God was still being extended.

After arriving in Toledo, Jerry found work at the Chemical-Lima Company, which was a transportation company operating in the area. The Chemical-Lima group specialized in transporting various food-grade and edible oils such as soybean oil, peanut oil, and other vegetable oils, as well as raw milk. Jerry's main job was cleaning the tanker trailers after delivery runs were completed. Chemical-Lima had to meet stringent health department standards in order to be a food-grade oil transporter. Because of round-the-clock operations, Jerry worked a swing shift arrangement that included working at night. His work times were coordinated to meet the needs of Chemical-Lima's shipping schedules.

During that time, he lived in the nearby town of Woodville, which was considered by some as a suburb of Toledo. With nothing to do during his off-duty time, he eagerly sought suitable places to fulfill his desire for a social life dominated by drinking and wild parties. Jerry always seemed to have a knack for finding where the action was, regardless of where he was living. It was no different in Toledo. He soon found a group to drink and party with and he exercised his desires in both situations to the fullest extent.

One cold night after a noticeable snowfall, Jerry and several of his rowdy friends were having a raucous party that became so loud and disorderly that the police raided it. At the appearance of the policemen, the partygoers scattered to the four winds. Jerry ran also, but he got separated from the other members of the group and later found his way to a large house in the general area. He summoned up enough courage to knock on the door and ask for help. It turned out that a doctor lived in the house and that he was a Christian man. Jerry, obviously under the influence of alcohol, asked the doctor for help, and without hesitation, the doctor readily agreed to help him. Jerry then asked the doctor to drive him back to Woodville. The doctor, noting the condition of his visitor, immediately chose to take him to Woodville as requested, and as a good Christian, used his time with Jerry to witness to him about the saving grace of Jesus Christ. The doctor delivered Jerry to the plant where he worked. Because he was to work an early shift the next morning, Jerry climbed into the

46

cab of a truck parked on the yard to get a little sleep and sober up before having to report for work. The driver, who happened to be sitting in the truck at the time, began to explain a problem with the steering mechanism of the vehicle. Thinking that Jerry was one of the company mechanics, the driver asked Jerry for his help in dealing with the faulty steering system. He told Jerry to drive the truck to get a firsthand look and the problem. Jerry, not thinking clearly at the time, agreed to test drive the truck. During the drive in about eight inches of snow, he lost control of the truck while driving too fast on the frozen streets and ran into the edge of the Ohio River. As the truck entered the water, he grabbed a post and extricated himself from the truck as it settled into the water. It was freezing weather and his clothes were soaked with water as he made his way back to the road. He started walking along the road to find help for the second time in the same night and quickly came upon a car sitting on the side of the road. The car was occupied by a group of Hispanic men who were drinking. He boldly climbed into the car in his wet clothes and asked the men if they would carry him home. Surprisingly, they agreed to his request and carried him to his home in Woodville. To Jerry's amazement, the sheriff came to his home the next morning and arrested him for stealing the truck, and proceeded with measures to take him to the county jail. He spent the next twenty-one days in jail before he could prove that he did not steal the truck.

While in the Toledo area, and shortly before the supposedly stolen truck incident, Jerry had an experience that later proved to be prophetic about God's future plans for him. While sleeping, he had a dream in which he was going about knocking on the doors of homes in a town and asking the occupants of those homes if he could tell them about Jesus Christ. In the dream, he was wearing a ministerial robe. Jerry, fearing that people would belittle the dream story and possibly make sport of him because of it, has never discussed this incident with anyone until very recently. When he was later called to be one of God's ministers, he recalled that dream he had so vividly experienced several years before. He feels that God was giving him a brief vision of what he was supposed to do for God in the future. He feels that, through his ministry, he was to knock on the doors of sinners' hearts and present the Good News of Jesus Christ. Later experiences in his ministry validate this aspect of God's calling to Jerry Ross.

Upon being released from jail, Jerry was briefly employed at a local lime plant in the Toledo area. After surviving the potentially serious accident with the company truck with nothing worse than wet clothes and hurt feelings, he was convinced that he was pushing his luck and that he should return to his home in the South, settle down, and get his life in order. Being in financial straits after the jail time, Jerry did not have a car for the trip south or the money for the needed bus ticket. After working at the lime plant for a few weeks, he was able to save up the price of a bus ticket to Alabama. After doing so, he bought the ticket and headed for Alabama and hopefully a better life.

Back home in Alabama, Jerry began to look more seriously at certain events that had occurred during his school years and at experiences endured during military service in Vietnam, as well as new civilian endeavors after his army time. That serious look at himself began to temper his self-evaluation and the image he had been projecting in his daily life. He began to discreetly alter the macho image he had been projecting to others for several years. He felt a need to shed the "tough guy" image he had worked so hard to develop in the past and to fit in with those friends and family with whom he was now associating. He was developing an innate desire to be looked upon as a good person; the life of the party, so to speak. Jerry was beginning to think about his past sinful lifestyle and to be concerned about himself and the life he was living.

Deep within, Jerry knew that he must make a change because he also realized that he owed the Heavenly Father a tremendous debt of gratitude for protecting him and for His grace, love, and patience that had been extended so many times. Although he was still unwilling to give his heart to God, he was beginning to fully and clearly recognize the certainty that he was back home safe and sound only through grace extended to him by a loving and patient God. Mistakenly, Jerry thought that he could please God by being good, and he slyly began to be a better person after he was once again at home with his parents. He was more discreet while practicing some of the old vices that he was unwilling to give up as he began to work on his newly chosen image of being good in an unobtrusive way. Although Jerry was trying to do better in many ways, he was still being pursued diligently by the Holy Spirit and His convicting power. In working to improve his image, Jerry Ross was trying to gain the peace of mind and heart by good works. He was yet to learn that salvation could not be bought by works, nor could true peace and happiness be obtained by anything but the shed blood of Jesus Christ. He now knows that good works alone will not suffice in man's quest for salvation.

Shortly after arriving back at his parents' home near Boaz, Alabama, Jerry once again found employment at the Boaz Spinning Mill. He had briefly worked there prior to his military service. One of his friends, Paul Crutchfield, was the third-shift foreman at the mill and was instrumental in the hiring of Ross for a production job in the plant. Although Jerry regained some seniority from his previous employment at the mill, he still did not rate the day shift any time except on special assignments. The graveyard shift was his basic assignment.

Paul Crutchfield was a bi-vocational pastor of Hill Church, a rural church in the Etowah County area, and as such, took a special interest in Jerry. Crutchfield knew something of Jerry's lifestyle and had a burning desire and burden to see him mend his ways and accept Christ into his heart and life. Pastor Crutchfield made it a point to come by the lunchroom and talk to Jerry during lunch and break periods. He didn't miss an opportunity to tell Jerry about the Good News of Jesus and the plan of salvation and how there was help and strength in Jesus. Another friend and fellow employee, Jimmy Mack Tarvin, also witnessed to Jerry during lunch periods and breaks. Both of those men continued to tell him the Good News of the plan of salvation and how Jesus could help him. Whereas Jerry would not listen to such talk in the past, he now had gotten to the place in his life that he was willing to listen as someone told him about the better life. Even with that mellowing of his attitude and demeanor, he still could not imagine himself as totally giving up his "good times" life. He felt that a dedicated Christian lifestyle would severely hamper his entertainment activities. He did not realize that turning his life over to God would open the doors to true happiness, joy, and contentment. Nor did he realize that a loving God would help him find peace, joy, and contentment once he walked through those doors. Jerry Ross was approaching the age of twenty-three years at the time all these thoughts were running through his mind. To thicken the plot of his life, he had just met a young lady named Darlene King who would later become his wife.

The circumstances surrounding the first meeting of Jerry Ross and Darlene King provide an interesting story. Jerry was interested in meeting and dating a nice young lady, but he also wanted to keep his rowdy past a secret from her. He feared that she would not go out with him if she learned about the rough life he had lived up to that time. Jerry had confided to a fellow third-shift worker that he would like to find a girl who would date him. The fellow worker told him that she would arrange a blind date for him with a person she knew. Having had some unsatisfactory experiences on some previous blind dates and having a vision of a fat, loud, and dominating person for his date, Jerry refused the offer. He asked the fellow worker, however, to continue to help him find a suitable date. One night at a later time, Jerry and his fellow worker were taking a break near the punch clock when Jerry noticed an attractive young lady punching in for work. He was immediately smitten by her and said to the fellow worker, "Do you see that pretty girl at the clock? Now there's the type of person I would really like to date. Do you think you could possibly get me a date with her?"

The fellow worker replied, "Jerry, that girl is the one who would have been your blind date if you had listened to me!"

Jerry, who always met strangers easily, went directly to the lady at the clock and immediately blurted out, "Will you marry me?" The young lady, completely thunderstruck by his forthrightness and highly unusual move, did not accept his sudden proposal. She did agree to a date at a later time and thus began the long-lasting relationship of Darlene King and Jerry Ross. It is interesting to note that the fellow worker who brought them together was Doris King, Darlene's aunt.

Darlene King was a quiet and unassuming young lady who wanted to do the right thing in whatever situation she was in. She was also a dedicated Christian who believed in going to church and living a life that was pleasing in God's sight. She and Jerry were polar opposites at the time. Darlene liked to go to church and Jerry didn't like to go; Darlene was a Christian, Jerry was not; Darlene was quiet and reserved and Jerry was loud and boisterous; Jerry enjoyed the seamy side of life and Darlene enjoyed the pleasures provided by living a Christian life. But, as in nature where like poles of a magnet repel each other, the unlike poles of a magnet have a very strong attraction for each other. This seemed to be the case with Jerry and Darlene. They were drawn to each other by their differences. God had to be a major player in this situation. After doing all the other things for Jerry, He was providing him with a future wife who would

50

be instrumental in leading him to Christ and then becoming a steadying influence and supporter in his future work.

After their momentous meeting at the Cotton Mill punch clock, Jerry and Darlene began to see each other on a fairly regular basis. Occasionally they would go to a fast-food establishment and have breakfast together after leaving the plant at the end of another shift. At other times when they were not working, they enjoyed each other's company by doing the simple and good things of life; sometimes visiting friends and family or going to a movie and at other times eating out. Many of their dates, at Darlene's insistence, were spent going to various church services together. Jerry was more than willing to push his reluctance for church attendance aside for a chance to be with Darlene. Sometimes they attended regular church services and at other times they attended revival services at nearby churches.

During that period of his life, Jerry Ross was being constantly bombarded by the combined forces of the good side of life. Pastor Paul Crutchfield, his foreman, was proactive in exposing him to the plan of salvation. Jimmy Mack Tarvin and other worker friends were equally persistent in their personal witness to Jerry as they tried to explain the plan of salvation to him. Jerry was willing to listen because he and Jimmy Mack had been friends since childhood and had always talked their problems out with each other. Jerry was impressed by the sincerity of Jimmy Mack and others as they explained to him about the source of peace, comfort, and satisfaction that was available to him if he would believe. Then there was his relationship with Darlene and the influence of the Christian example she was living before him. Lastly, the Holy Spirit was a constant companion with Jerry as He increased the convicting pressure on him. It was obvious that God was doing everything possible to capture Jerry's attention. Then, as he looked back on his life and remembered all the times that God had brought him safely through extremely dangerous situations in Vietnam, Ohio, and other places, he was reminded of the numerous promises he had made to God and then promptly broken. The combination of all those factors had created such a load on him that he was beginning to feel the absolute necessity of making a change. Although much of his ingrained reluctance was still present, his resistance to God was beginning to fade away. Getting right with God was becoming a case of "when," not "if" for Jerry Ross. Today, he summarizes the situation very succinctly when he says, "I felt for certain that this was the last chance that God was going to give me. If I failed Him again, it would be my last time and I would be eternally lost."

As time progressed, his parents' home church conducted its annual revival during the summer of 1968. Pleasant Hill Church, near Boaz, Alabama, was a Southern Baptist Church and was served pastorally by a friend of the Ross family, the Reverend Bueman Owens. Reverend Crutchfield and Jimmy Mack Tarvin, who were members of the Pleasant Hill community, talked to Jerry at work before the upcoming revival and once again witnessed to him about his need for Christ to be in his life. They issued a special invitation to him to attend the revival next week and, at their insistence, he promised them that he would attend at least some of the services. Jerry's parents were also determined and insistent that he would attend the revival. Many others, including family members and friends, were praying for his salvation at the time.

Jerry relates an interesting story about some of the prayers that were offered on his behalf and how they were answered in a very timely fashion. He was still working third shift, which ended at seven o'clock in the morning. His usual routine was to go to bed after arriving home and eating, and then sleep until late afternoon. Sometime before the revival week began, he started waking up at about ten o'clock in the morning for some unexplained reason. He would be wringing wet with perspiration and would be smothering for breath. There were no obvious noises such as TV sets, radios, or telephones present to awaken him at that particular time. What really ground on Jerry's nerves was the fact that he could never go back to sleep after those abrupt awakenings. The answer to the problem was revealed to him in a few days when he was talking to Reverend Crutchfield at work. During the conversation, Crutchfield stated that he had been praying for Jerry to be saved. He told Jerry that he had been beseeching God to do whatever it took to bring Jerry into the fold. He had asked God to take his appetite, keep him from sleeping, and whatever else it took to get Jerry saved before it was too late. Although Jerry did not tell the Reverend Crutchfield, he now knew the reason for his sleeplessness. As he considered the reason for his sleep problem, the reason for another problem was revealed. All of a sudden, the bountiful lunches Jerry's mother packed for him did not seem appetizing to him at all. Rather than try to force them down, he would stop at a fast-food place and buy something for lunch. Those bought lunches did not appeal to him either. It finally dawned on him that he was under deeper conviction because of answered prayers.

In those days, it was customary for most rural churches to have morning and night services, and revivals always lasted at least a week. During the afternoons of the revival and sometimes before the revival, the pastor and the evangelist visited in the community with particular attention being given to the lost people of the community. On that particular occasion, the pastor, the Reverend Bueman Owens, along with several of the deacons, had been visiting in the community that week for the purposes of witnessing and inviting people to the revival.

On Friday night before the week of Pleasant Hill's revival, Paul Crutchfield talked to Jerry while both were at work and told him that he and Reverend Owens would visit him on Saturday. When Brother Crutchfield asked him what time he got up, Jerry stated that he usually got up about two o'clock. Reverend Crutchfield advised him that they would come to visit him at that time. Later, it dawned on Jerry what he had said, and he immediately began to devise a way to get out of the appointment. He told his mother to awaken him at noon that Saturday. Jerry feared that he might sleep beyond the ten o'clock time at which he had been waking up during recent days. He then retired for his sleep time, believing he had solved the problem of avoiding the preachers' visit. His motive was to get up, get dressed, and get away from the house before the group of preachers and deacons arrived. Jerry didn't know it, but the plan he had devised was about to go awry. The day was Saturday, August 10, 1968, and Jerry's life was to be changed forever. After all those years of striving with Jerry Ross, God and the Holy Spirit were about to win the battle and Jerry was to gain victory in his heart, soul, and mind.

Mrs. Ruby Ross looked in on her son at noon that day and found him to be sleeping so soundly that she decided to let him sleep on; she knew he needed the rest, especially since he had definitely not been sleeping well for several days. Unaware of Jerry's plan to leave the house before the preachers arrived, she decided not to disturb him. He was still sleeping when his father awakened him with some alarming news. Mr. Ross told Jerry that the preachers and deacons had arrived about one thirty in the afternoon. Learning that Jerry was still asleep, they told Mr. Ross that they would briefly visit at another home and would be back in ten to fifteen minutes. Upon learning of the impending visit, Jerry jumped from the bed and began to make hasty preparations to get dressed and leave before the group returned. After brushing his teeth and combing his hair, he began hunting his clothes and immediately had trouble finding the ones he wanted. Jerry fancied himself a smart dresser and one who wanted his clothes to be properly color-coordinated and matched. To begin with, he couldn't find the shirt or trousers he was hunting. In his haste, he remained unable to find his chosen clothes. He says now that he feels God had something to do with his inability to find the clothes as a part of a delaying tactic to prevent him from standing the preachers up. He even asked his mother if she had moved his clothes and she replied that she had not. Miraculously, he suddenly found all of the clothes he had been overlooking. By the time he was finally able to get dressed, it was only three or four minutes until the expected return of the church group. By that time, it was fast becoming apparent that God was about to win the battle for Jerry's life. For the first time, he could almost hear the voice of God saying, "Come unto me and find the joy!"

After hurriedly dressing, Jerry walked out onto the front porch of his parents' house with every intention of leaving the scene. It was not to be, however, because the church group pulled into the driveway at the same time. Oddly, perhaps intentionally, they parked one of their cars directly behind Jerry's car that was in the middle of the driveway. He thought that was unusual at the time, especially since it was a large yard with plenty of space for several cars. He feels that his visitors must have prayed before coming back to his house and that God may have revealed his escape plans to them. He says that he hopes to ask them about it someday.

After the usual greetings and exchange of pleasantries, there was some small talk about old memories, growing up, and other things they had experienced. They even talked about some things in Jerry's life. Those lighthearted comments led up to the real reason for the visit. One of the members of the group looked Jerry in the eye and said, "Jerry, we have come to see you saved. You've told us with your own words that you have never been saved and that you were going to die and go to hell. We don't want to see that happen right here near the door of the church and in this community." Jerry states that he remembers the group's comments almost word for word to this day. He was impressed with the fact that the group did not criticize him because of his past. Rather, they expressed their Christian love for him and the fact that he needed Christ in his life.

Following those preliminary remarks, the group bowed there in the front yard and prayed.

When the prayer was finished, Reverend Bueman Owens put his arm around Jerry and asked, "Jerry, do you feel any different? Are you saved?"

Jerry replied, "No, I feel relieved about some of the things I confessed."

Brother Owens said, "I heard you, but you never did ask the Lord to come into your heart and be your Savior. You were trying to justify your life and get it approved before you get saved." Brother Owens talked more to Jerry in a calm and serious manner. He and Jerry bowed and prayed again, with Jerry thinking that rockets would go off, bells would ring, thunder would roll, and other spectacular things would happen at the time of salvation. It didn't happen that way for him. At the conclusion of the second prayer, Jerry rose up and saw a completely different and beautiful world. It seemed that everything had changed. The summertime colors had a new brilliance; the skies were a brighter blue; even the people looked different to him. Reverend Owens asked him if he had been saved.

Jerry started to reply, "I think I'm saved," and almost choked. He then said, "I'm saved!" He now says that it felt like all the joy in heaven had been poured out on him. A terrific load had been lifted and replaced with an indescribable happiness and joy. It was indeed a marvelous time when Jerry Ross finally sought and accepted the deliverance that a loving God had been trying to give him for years. Now, as a person who has "been there and done that," he urges people not to wait as he did in refusing the pleadings of the Holy Spirit for so long. Although he knows that our loving God is patient and forgiving, he also knows that the Holy Spirit will not always strive with man.

Some of the first people Jerry saw after he accepted Christ as his Savior were his parents. They had witnessed the entire episode of Jerry's conversion. His mother came running to him with outstretched arms, shouting all the way and praising the Lord. His father, a six-foot-six-inch-tall man with only a fringe of hair, was crying unashamedly at the sight of his newly saved son. Jerry had never seen his father cry before. It was truly a happy time for the Ross family. Jerry now realized what loving and

55

great people his parents were. His appreciation of them knew no bounds once he saw them in that light. All the past heartaches, tears, arguments, and fights brought on them by Jerry were forgiven and forgotten. It was a time of great rejoicing for the Ross family. Truly, that son who was lost was now found.

Even though Jerry was now saved, the persistent Paul Crutchfield would not let up on him. Paul reminded him that the Pleasant Hill Baptist Church's revival was running the very next week and that Jerry should be there. Jerry reminded Paul that he was working third shift and that he needed to get some rest, and as a result, he didn't know if he could attend revival or not. Besides that, now that he was saved, he was able to sleep like a baby.

His friends kept talking about the revival, and after thinking about the invitation to attend the revival, Jerry remembered that he had not attended a revival since childhood and didn't really know what went on at revivals. He went to his friend, Jimmy Mack Tarvin, and asked, "Jimmy, what goes on at a revival now? Do they walk the floor, pull and push, and that kind of stuff?"

Jimmy replied, "Oh no, they sing a bunch of songs, testify and have preaching, give an altar call, and go home."

Finally deciding that he should go to the revival, Jerry asked his friend, "Jimmy, can I go to revival with you and your wife on Tuesday night? I'll come by and pick you up."

Jimmy said, "Yeah, come by and we'll go with you."

Tuesday came and Jerry attended the revival service not really knowing what to expect. He seated himself near the back of the church and was soon joined by his friend, Jimmy Mack Tarvin and his wife. The service commenced, the spirit started to move, and Jerry's heart began to pound within his chest. The Lord, through the Spirit, was urging him to stand and tell what God had done for him on the previous Saturday, and that his lifestyle had changed. Jerry replied, "Lord, I don't know what to say." He was concerned about testifying and reluctant to do so because there were people present that night who were familiar with his previous rough and rowdy life. He continued, "Lord, if you are real and I've got the right feeling that I think I've got, let Jimmy Mack Tarvin stand and testify."

Jimmy Mack, a devout Christian, was not one to stand and testify publicly, even though he was very willing and ready to witness to lost people. Within two minutes, Tarvin stood and said that he loved the Lord and that he was proud he was saved and a part of the community. Then he sat down. To Jerry's amazement, God had very quickly responded to his request and had put the ball directly in his court; now the next move was up to him.

Jerry's uncle Elmer Ross, who was directing the singing for the revival, said, "I feel like someone else needs to say something." Those words really applied the pressure to Jerry as the Lord continued to prod him to testify. At that point, he felt for an instant that his newfound peace was about to be taken from him.

He said, "Wait, Lord, I want to keep that peace." With that, he stood up to testify as best he could, but without really knowing what to say. Jerry then told all those present, "I don't really know what to say and I don't know if you know it, but I got saved by the Grace of God last Saturday." He then sat down and was startled when several people stood and began to shout and praise God for what they had heard. Jerry, who felt at the time that he had been the chief among sinners, didn't really understand what was going on. He thought that what had happened to him was of a private nature and would remain that way, but he soon came to realize that those people knew all about what he was going through because they had been through the same thing themselves. Almost immediately after the revival, Jerry joined Pleasant Hill Baptist Church after very strong leadership from God to join that church.

Following his conversion experience, Jerry immediately began to attend church on a regular basis. He and his girlfriend Darlene went to church together most Sundays and sometimes on Wednesday nights. They truly enjoyed each other's company and spent every possible moment together. They worked together, went out to eat together, and went to church together. At first, they split their churchgoing time between Jerry's church, Pleasant Hill Baptist Church, and Darlene's church, New Union First Congregational Methodist Church. That plan continued for a short time after they were married on September 14, 1968. The plan worked out well for a time, but Jerry felt that God had a special reason for leading him to join the Pleasant Hill Church and that both of them should be in the same church. He also felt that their Bible study and spiritual growth would be more meaningful and fulfilling if they were in the same church. While the churches were very similar in many aspects, there were some

57

minor differences in the doctrines and procedures. Jerry did not want any of those differences to create even the smallest division in his and Darlene's married life. He felt that God wanted to plant them in a church together and to put the two of them on a solid Christian foundation together. He and Darlene talked and prayed about the situation for a time and he finally asked her to join Pleasant Hill Baptist Church.

While seeking a satisfactory solution to the situation, they went to talk with Jerry's uncle Elmer Ross, who was a deeply dedicated Christian and was very knowledgeable about the operation of the church. Uncle Elmer explained the rules for joining Pleasant Hill Baptist Church, with particular emphasis on requirements for those candidates for membership who were coming from other denominations. He explained that Pleasant Hill would accept the baptism of those coming from sister Baptist churches, but those coming from other denominations had to be baptized as a requirement for membership in Pleasant Hill Church. Darlene commented that she had been baptized by immersion at New Union F.C.M. Church by the Reverend H. L. Wofford, and that she was happy with her baptism. She did not feel that she should be re-baptized, and she rejected the idea of such a requirement at the time. Uncle Elmer then remarked, "If the Lord is leading you to join, Darlene, let Brother Bueman or someone else of your choice baptize you and live with what you've got in your heart, but do what it takes to keep the family together." Jerry, knowing Darlene's determination, felt that she would not go that route, but he kept praying that God would help to resolve the issue.

As time passed and Jerry continued to pray that Darlene would join Pleasant Hill Church with him, they continued to attend both their churches on an alternating basis. This type of church attendance, while serving God in a number of ways, was not what either of them wanted. It was hard to put down roots, build on a firm foundation, and grow spiritually with such an arrangement. Two months later, while they were attending services at Pleasant Hill, God answered Jerry's prayers. During the service, Darlene stood up to say something and began to cry. Brother Owens said, "It's time, isn't it?" Darlene replied, "Yes." Although she didn't feel that she was joining the church as a candidate for baptism, she told Jerry that although she was perfectly satisfied with her previous baptism, she wanted to become a member of Pleasant Hill Church to keep them together as they served God in their marriage. They both felt that God was founding them in the faith and preparing them for the work they would face in the future as a team.

With the resolution of that issue, Jerry and Darlene were ready to move into the future with a solid confidence founded on a strong faith in God. They both developed a great hunger for the Word of God and a thirst for knowledge of God's plan for them. To satisfy those desires, they began attending many revival meetings throughout the Sand Mountain area, in addition to all the services at their home church. Although he had not revealed it to anyone at the time, Jerry knew that God had already given him the call to preach the Word. Not only had God called Jerry to preach, He gave him the plan. Jerry knew he was to preach; he was to pastor churches; he was to work directly with sinners; he was to go into the field and into the highways and hedges and seek the lost. Today, he still feels that a major compelling work in a Christian's life in God's kingdom is in the highways and hedges in the immediate areas of present-day churches. While Jerry knows that the gospel must be carried into all the world as directed in the Great Commission, he feels that there is a great work to be done near local churches. That great work can take root in a local church and then spread to the far reaches of the Earth.

Realizing and burdened by all those directions from God, Jerry was ready and anxious to get to the work at hand. The full realization that this was a definite calling from God shook him to his life's foundation and quickly settled on Jerry and then, just a suddenly, became his guideline in life. He knew that he was to preach God's Word and that the time to start was immediately. During this period of time, he had an experience that was supernatural in nature and one that tested him to the limit. It also made his calling so plain to him that it left no doubt whatsoever in his mind. The supernatural incident occurred after his marriage and while he was still working third shift at the local cotton mill. In addition to the time requirements of his job, he was attending Gadsden State Community College at the time. His usual routine was to come home from work in the mornings, eat breakfast, and then dress and leave for school in early enough to be on time for his classes.

One morning as he was leaving the city of Boaz on his way to Gadsden State, a traffic light that was green very suddenly turned to red, causing Jerry to have to brake very hard to stop his vehicle without running the light. As he was stopping, he noticed an unkempt hitchhiker standing by

59

the road with his belongings stuffed into a large duffel bag. The hitchhiker was wearing beads and rough fatigue clothing and was sporting a five- or six-day growth of beard. He definitely was not very pleasing to look at. While looking at the man, Jerry said that the sweet voice of God spoke to him very clearly and said, "That man over there needs a ride." Jerry immediately began to offer excuses for not wanting to give the man a ride. He rationalized in his mind that he didn't need to take a chance with an unkempt person riding in the car with him to Gadsden. He came up with a list of several reasons why he should pass up the hitchhiker. While Jerry was completing his list of reasons for passing up the hitchhiker, God spoke to him again and said, "Stop! Let him ride." He clearly understood God's command and pulled to a stop and told the hitchhiker to get in.

The hitchhiker got in to the car and told Jerry his name. Jerry asked him, "Are you from around here?" The man replied, "No, I am not from here. I am just going to Atlanta." Jerry explained that he was only going to Gadsden and that his rider should follow Highway 431 through Anniston to Interstate 20 and then take it to Atlanta. The hitchhiker then stated that he appreciated the information.

Once the two were underway to Gadsden, God spoke to Jerry again and said, "You've never seen him before and you'll never see him again. See if you really want to preach." Jerry began to talk to his rider about Christianity, and the stranger quietly agreed with what he was saying. The Lord prodded Jerry again and said, "Preach." He had been carefully studying the Bible for some time and had learned things from the Bible that he could share with his passenger. He began to do so and, in the process, he started to actually preach to the hitchhiker and continued to do so until they started down the mountain on Highway 431 just north of Attalla, Alabama. The passenger listened quietly and with little comment as they rode toward Gadsden. As they were going down the mountain toward Attalla, the man interrupted Jerry from his impromptu preaching and said to him, "If you don't care, pull over and let me out at the intersection of highways 431 and 278. I am not going to Atlanta. I'll go to Cullman." Jerry was puzzled because the man had just told him shortly before that he really knew nothing about Alabama and that he was going to Atlanta, but it didn't really register on Jerry's mind about the sudden change of direction and destination of the hitchhiker. Upon reaching the intersection, Jerry pulled over and let the man out of the car and wished him well in his travels. Still puzzled by the sudden change of events, Jerry mused to himself, "Well, I made such a mess of that, the man wouldn't even finish his ride." At that time, Jerry began to fully realize that God was indeed calling him to preach.

As Jerry pulled back onto the highway, God spoke to him yet another time, saying, "Look in your rearview mirror." He looked into the mirror, and to his great astonishment, there was absolutely no one in sight anywhere, even at the site where he had just discharged his passenger. Unable to believe his eyes, he carefully looked again and there still was no one to be seen at or even near the place where he had just let his passenger out of the car. As he began to move away from the scene of the mystery, it was quite evident to Jerry that the man could not have gotten into another car, since no cars were to be seen at the place. As he tried to sort out what his unbelieving eyes had just seen, Jerry recalled a scripture that he had recently studied, and was immediately convinced that he had just entertained a heavenly visitor. In Hebrews 13:2, the Bible says, "Be not forgetful to entertain strangers; for thereby some have entertained angels unawares." Jerry says of that encounter, "God sent an angel to convince me that I was on the right path. I believe that until today." At that time, Jerry began to fully realize that God was indeed calling him to preach. He feels not only that his encounter with the mysterious passenger was a test administered by God, but it was also a confirmation of his call to preach the Word of God. The episode succeeded in putting the fear of God into him; so much, in fact, that he wouldn't tell anyone about what happened for at least a week. About a week later—still reluctant to announce his calling to preach the Word—Jerry had to tell his wife Darlene the details of what had happened to him on that fateful trip to Gadsden, Alabama.

Once he had told her about his experience with the hitchhiker, Darlene related what God had revealed to her. She said, "The Lord has shown me that we have a lot of work to do." That was all she said at the time. Jerry was fervently hoping that she would say that she knew he had been called to preach and was right with the Lord and it was all right for him to go ahead and announce his calling and then handle what he had to do, but she stopped short of saying that. In a sense of the word, it seemed to Jerry that he was left out on a limb with the decision he was going to be required to make. The problem now was how to keep from sawing the limb off between himself and the tree. The pressure to announce his call-

61

ing was becoming greater by the day, and he felt that he needed help in dealing with the situation. Feeling that some of his minister friends who had been through the same type of thing would be a source of help in ascertaining exactly what his calling was, Jerry began to consult with them for answers, without realizing at the time that the One who had called him had the answers he needed.

Shortly thereafter, he began to visit with some of his preacher friends to seek their advice on how to handle his situation. While doing so, he set up a hypothetical situation in his mind wherein a person, presumably Jerry's friend, had been called to preach but was concerned about the work he would have to do as a God-called minister. When Jerry presented his "friend's" case to Reverend James Perigo, Brother Perigo bluntly stated, "If that friend of yours that God has called to His work is too sorry to work and doesn't want to work, tell him to suffer." Jerry states that Reverend Perigo knew who the friend was.

Later, Jerry visited with the Reverend Arthur Davis, a respected and trusted friend, to present the hypothetical case to him and to get his input on it. Reverend Davis, affectionately known to his multitude of friends as Uncle Arthur, boldly said, "Son, I can't tell you anything, but go back and tell that friend if he ever wants peace, joy, and tranquility with the Lord, he is going to have to be obedient unto Him, but tell him if he doesn't, don't come back and bother me." Brother Davis also saw through Jerry's façade about the "friend." In reality, it was revealed to both men that Jerry was the "friend." He then consulted several other preacher friends about his situation, but none of them would confirm or tell him that he was called to preach.

Still seeking confirmation of his call, Jerry and Darlene began to attend revivals at various churches on a very regular basis. All the time, he was grasping at straws in a vain effort to satisfy himself that he was truly called to preach. He felt certain that he had the call, but the evil one continued to place doubts in his mind. Once again, however, God was slowly but surely winning the battle.

One of the revival visits was made to a church called Hill Church. During the very spiritual service, the evangelist, Reverend Charlie Bouldin and his wife Geneva were singing a song titled "The Rock that Was Hewed out of the Mountain." The song has a very profound message and is quite moving as it is presented. As depicted in the song, the Holy Bible is the Rock and the lyrics tell of a search for the Rock that is eventually found. Throughout the song, the singers were looking in various places in the church for the Bible and they finally found it and placed it on the pulpit. Then, to Jerry's dismay, Brother Bouldin picked up the Bible and began to walk in Jerry's direction. He had indescribable feelings as Brother Bouldin walked by and placed the Bible in his hands. This turned out to be the clarion call for Jerry to announce his calling. He arose to testify and get some relief, and wound up preaching for about five minutes, during which he said for all to hear, "I know God has called me to preach and I want to do the best I can."

When Jerry had finished, three young girls came to the altar. Their ages were about twelve, fourteen, and sixteen years. He thinks one of them may have been a church member at the time. Collectively, they stated that they had never been saved, but after praying through, they were now saved. God spoke to Jerry and told him that if he would mind Him, follow Him, and believe Him, He would bless him. That was a valuable and well-learned lesson for Jerry and one that would be a guideline in the future.

Following the experience at Hill Church, Jerry was back in his home church. The word was out that he had announced his calling during a revival service at the Hill Church. He was immediately given an appointment to preach at his church. It is a custom in most country churches that men who have announced their calling to preach the gospel will be given an invitation to preach at their home churches at the earliest possible date. On the appointed date of Jerry's first message at Pleasant Hill, he and Darlene arrived to find a full house. Several members of Darlene's family were present for the service, as was most of Jerry's family. Many of those people had been working with him for years and praying and asking God to save him. As Jerry looked at the large crowd and pondered the situation, Satan began to put doubts in his mind by saying, "Now, since you are so intelligent and inspired, let's see you preach tonight." Jerry was scared to death of the situation but determined to do his best. At the appointed time in the service, the pastor, Reverend "Doc" Tidwell, called him to the pulpit and Jerry, still in shock because of the large crowd, stammered, "Do you mean me?"

Brother Tidwell went ahead and turned the service over to him, saying, "Now it is time, come on and give us what God has given you." He began to deliver the message that God had given him, as Satan continued

63

to tell him that he'd fall flat on this face. Jerry's first sermon at his home church, Pleasant Hill Baptist Church, was not a long one, probably five to eight minutes in length, but God blessed the service and the efforts of His new servant. At the conclusion of the message, one person came forward seeking salvation, prayed through, and was saved. Once again, God had come through for Jerry.

A great transformation had occurred in the life of Jerry Ross. In his teenage years, early working years, and army years, he had been a "macho" man. He felt that he was self-sufficient within himself and was totally able to fend for himself, regardless of the situation. Although he was raised in a dedicated Christian home, he continually pushed God aside for many years and resisted His efforts to change his life. Even though he was Satan's servant in those times, Jerry experienced some decent times initially. As time passed, however, problems began to raise their ugly heads and things were not as pleasant as he would like.

Jerry's experiences in the Armed Services had a profound effect on him. The war in Vietnam—a very unpopular war in the United States— produced a generation of veterans who were very reluctant to discuss the war once they returned to the States. Although a vast majority of them supported the Vietnam action and were committed to the United States' involvement in the issue, they did not feel at ease discussing it publicly back home because of the vast undercurrent of opposition to the war at home. Jerry, a highly decorated veteran of the Vietnam War, shared the concern and actions of his contemporaries and chose not to discuss his many contributions to the war effort. To this day, many of his friends and acquaintances have no idea whatsoever about his exploits while serving in a war zone.

While Jerry was an active participant in all the military battles that were going on around him in the Republic of South Vietnam, there was a tremendous battle between the forces of good and evil going on in his spiritual being. As a result of close calls he experienced in Vietnam, Jerry began to call on God in particularly perilous times and to ask Him for His protection. As an extra facet of his request for protection and deliverance, he would underscore the prayers with promises to do better in the future, to get his life in the proper lane, to seek salvation, and to tell the world about it. His life was a tangle of broken promises to God from that time up to the time he was saved. He was seeking peace, but was really in a perpetual state of unrest and worry up to that time.

Once Jerry was saved and had joined the church, he found that peace, joy, and contentment that he had been seeking all those years. He answered God's call to preach the gospel and was ready and willing to embark on a new journey—a journey on which God would be the leader and captain. Jerry was ready to be one of God's messengers and for God's will to be done in his life. He fully realized that he had reached that point only through grace and the mercy of God. Jerry was now ready to enter a new phase of life as a God-called minister who would probably pastor churches and as one who would go into the highways and byways seeking the lost and bringing them to Christ.

Chapter 4

The Jerry Ross Ministry
Serving and Glorifying God

A new day had dawned in the life of Jerry Ross. He had finally accepted Christ as his Lord and Savior and was beginning a totally new phase of work as he came to grips with the demands of his calling. The peace, joy, and contentment he now felt as a Christian far exceeded anything he could have ever imagined in the turbulent life that he had led prior to his becoming a Christian. He had sought peace and joy in all the wrong places and for the wrong reasons as he lived his worldly life. He learned the hard way that alcohol and the other worldly pleasures could not give lasting peace, joy, and contentment, and that pursuit of worldly pleasures merely added to his discontent and unhappiness at the time. He now realizes that those years spent in serving the world were indeed wasted years and that they were time spent very foolishly and definitely for the wrong purpose.

Even while he was yet a sinner, Jerry felt that God might have special work for him to do. He just didn't know for sure what the work was. Shortly after Jerry became a Christian, God revealed to him that his mission was to preach the Word. After a short period of personal doubt about his suitability for God's work, the Heavenly Father gave Jerry a couple of profound encounters that convinced him that God had made no mistake

67

in calling him to preach. The first was when Jerry picked up the hitch-hiker and the second was when he announced his calling and preached a brief sermon during a revival at the Hill Church. Jerry did what God requested him to do in each case and found out firsthand that obedience to God brings unspeakable joy, contentment, and happiness—conditions the world cannot supply.

After the years of broken promises to God, Jerry was eager to make up for lost time in his service to God. He had filled a couple of appointments to preach shortly after announcing his calling and was yearning for more opportunities preach the Word. All the while, he was studying the Scriptures and preparing for future appointments that God might provide for him. Jerry felt that he should diligently search and study the Scriptures for his guidance in delivering the Word. God led Jerry to preach in a sedate manner while delivering his messages and to clearly and firmly present the gospel message in a way that could be understood by the vilest of sinners. Fully believing that all his sermons should be delivered as directed by the Holy Spirit, Jerry tried to complete them in about thirty minutes unless there was a special leading of the Spirit directing otherwise.

After the initial flurry of activity surrounding Jerry's accepting Christ and subsequently announcing his call to preach, there was a brief drought of invitations for Jerry to preach. He was concerned about that development and began to have doubts about his ministry. He knew that he had been called to preach and was starving to preach the Word. He began to wonder if something was wrong somewhere. He confided his concerns to Darlene and they prayed together about the situation while holding hands across a coffee table and over a large white family Bible. Jerry asked God to show him what was wrong at the present and what he should do to improve and be a better servant. Jerry asked God, if it was His will, to please give him the opportunity to preach. Miraculously, the phone rang about the time they were finishing the prayer. Even though it was late in the day, the call was a request to preach that very night. Jerry told the caller that, God willing, he would be more than glad to fill the request.

While Jerry and Darlene were dressing and making preparations to fulfill that night's appointment, the phone rang again. This time, it was a caller from another church, asking him to preach that night at *his* church. Jerry explained that he was already obligated for that night, but would be happy to visit and preach at a later date.

68

They booked a date for Jerry to preach at that church the following Sunday night. These events were a special lesson to Jerry Ross, in that he learned once again that calling upon God for help in times of need and turning problems over to Him was the only thing to do. He further learned that listening to Him when He replies and fully depending on Him for continued guidance can make the work so much easier and more successful.

After that time, he began to get appointments to preach at a number of churches. The churches where he filled appointments were scattered over a major part of northeast Alabama and northwest Georgia. Jerry filled appointments at Decatur, Alabama and at Cedartown, Rockmart, and one of the Atlanta suburbs in Georgia. He also preached at many of the local area Baptist churches and was blessed to be invited to preach to the congregations of churches of other denominations. Jerry felt that it was a special blessing from God to be honored with all those appointments. Filling them under God's leadership and provision was very uplifting to him, and he was very thankful to God for bringing him through so many dangerous situations to that present moment in time. Jerry was doubly blessed and thankful to see a number of sinners come to Christ and be saved in those early days of his ministry as he filled those guest preacher appointments.

One of those notable early appointments in his ministry occurred when Jerry was invited to preach at Sardis (Alabama) Baptist Church. The pastor, Reverend Scott Bryant, contacted Jerry and explained that he and his wife would be away on a certain Sunday for a brief vacation. He asked Jerry to preach for him on that Sunday, and Jerry readily agreed to do so. Then, Brother Bryant explained to Jerry that he meant for him to preach that Sunday night and the following Wednesday night also. Jerry was shocked by the request as he contemplated preparing and delivering three messages in such a short time. His concern increased noticeably as he considered that Sardis Baptist was a fairly large church, composed of a richly blessed congregation and that many of its members were family friends of long standing who were familiar with his past life. Remembering his promises to God, Jerry sought His help and leadership in preparation for the three services.

God anointed Jerry and he prepared and delivered the messages and then blessed the services from the very portals of heaven. During one of the services, a young girl came to the altar for prayer and then blessed Jerry immensely when she said, "I like you as a preacher. When you preached, I felt something, and beside that, you zipped through the message and were done. I like that." Jerry and his wife Darlene were pleasantly uplifted by the young lady's candor. Jerry isn't, and never has been, a long-winded type of preacher. Jerry received a great blessing from worshiping with many dear friends at Sardis Baptist Church.

As time went by, Jerry was invited to preach at many of the local churches. God had answered his prayer for opportunities to preach in a mighty way, and Jerry and Darlene praised Him for that. In fact, the invitations were coming at such a pace that his attendance at his home church, Pleasant Hill Baptist Church, became very sporadic. He preached at several local churches, including Mountainboro Baptist Church in the small Etowah County community of Mountainboro, Alabama.

While God was using him in filling a large number of appointments as a guest speaker in several local churches, Jerry had a burden and felt that he should be serving as a pastor in a church somewhere. Even though he had a burning desire to become a pastor in his ministry, God had other things in mind for Jerry. The previous opportunities to preach in a large number of churches and on the local radio stations had whetted his desire to become a pastor, and he questioned God and asked why he was not getting to pastor a church. God spoke and told him that he was not to be a pastor at the time, but that he would do pastoral work at a later time. Suddenly, the requests for Jerry to preach in the local churches dried up completely, and for a period of about two months, he didn't receive an invitation to speak anywhere. God used the dry spell in Jerry's preaching ministry to underscore the fact that Jerry was to humbly follow God's plan for his life and that he was not to try to upstage or modify God's plans for his life. Jerry feels that God was using those preaching appointments in a multitude of settings to broaden his experience as He trained him for the serious challenges and responsibilities associated with being a pastor.

During that two-month period, Jerry and Darlene talked and prayed about the matter. They said to each other, "Here we go again." There was time for them to think about and review God's plan for their lives. They became humble as they prayed and asked God for His leadership in their lives. They became willing for God's will, not theirs, to be done in their ministerial service to Him. They earnestly asked Him for new opportunities to serve Him, realizing all the while that it all must be by His leadership. Once they placed God and His work first, the doors of service to Him began to open again.

Very shortly, a pulpit committee from the Butler Baptist Church visited Jerry and asked him to come and preach for them as they sought a new pastor for their church. He filled the appointment and delivered the message God gave him. Some of the members of the church had also heard Jerry preach at a local radio station. In a later-called business session, the church conference called Jerry to be pastor of Butler Baptist Church. Jerry accepted the call and set out to be "about the Father's business."

Jerry's arrival on the field at Butler Baptist Church was somewhat of an eye-opener for him. Although there were good Christian folks in the church, there was not a closeness to the group, and attendance was very low. There was a coolness between some of the members at certain times and some testy situations of the past had been allowed to fester within the confines of the church. All of those situations were hindering the growth and operation of the church. With only about sixteen persons attending the church on a regular basis, one person had to fill several positions such as song director, Sunday school superintendent, teacher, and deacon.

Jerry met with that person, Dennis Oliver, to discuss the problems of the church and to formulate and install plans to unite the church and place it on the path to growth, harmony, and prosperity. Jerry, being a firm believer in missions work, told Dennis that he was firmly convinced that while a pastor had a heavy responsibility within a church, he also had very important work outside the church in the field and general area surrounding the church. He was convinced that a pastor must have a very obvious physical presence within the community of his pastorate. Not only should a pastor be out carrying the Good News of Jesus and inviting and encouraging people to come into His service, he should be seeking out and learning of needs and problems within the community that the church might minister to.

Brother Oliver was elated to hear what Jerry Ross, the new pastor of Butler Baptist Church, had said about being a viable part of the community. Upon hearing Jerry's remarks, Brother Oliver exclaimed, "Thank God that I am hearing you say that, because that's exactly the way I feel. Let's go!" Dennis Oliver had lived in the community for many years and knew most of the people therein. To a large degree, he was cognizant of the concerns that many members and non-members had regarding attending and working in the Butler church. Pastor Jerry Ross was thankful and happy to have the competent help of Dennis Oliver as they formulated plans to heal Butler Baptist and then began to put them in place.

The two of them—Brother Jerry and Brother Dennis—began a very proactive program of visitation and inquiry in their initial quest to "grow" the Butler Baptist Church back to the status it had enjoyed in previous years. They visited diligently in the community and knocked on every door in the process, but with little success at first. They were received well at a few homes, nonchalantly at others, and were even asked to leave at some other homes. Those experiences proved that a great deal of work would be required to restore the church to its previous standing.

Jerry and Dennis were persistent in their mission and refused to be discouraged by the negative aspect of it. Very slowly, their hard work began to pay off and more people started to attend Butler Baptist Church. Although the gains were slow, they were a positive response to their efforts and were a solid source of encouragement to them. Those small successes were a real blessing not only to Jerry and Dennis, but also to the congregation as a whole.

As time went by, additional opportunities for witnessing presented themselves. One of the first was when Dennis heard that a young girl in the community, Rhonda Taylor, was scheduled for major surgery in Birmingham Children's Hospital the next day. He contacted Jerry and told him about the impending surgery and the sad fact that she didn't have a pastor, deacon or other church member to be with her during her time of surgery. Since it was impossible for both of them to be there on the day of the surgery, Jerry suggested that they visit the patient in the hospital that very night. Immediately, they began preparations to go to the children's hospital that night.

When Jerry climbed into his old Buick LeSabre to pick Dennis up for the trip to Birmingham, he noticed that the car was so low on gasoline that it would be impossible to make the trip. Checking his pockets, he found that he only had about a dollar and a half, not nearly enough to buy gasoline for the trip. Jerry didn't know what to do except to turn the situation over to God. He went to his uncle Elmer's store and explained to him why he needed to go to Birmingham and the fact that he was out of gas. He would rather have taken a whipping than ask his uncle for help.

Uncle Elmer said, "Pull up to that pump, boy." Jerry asked for three dollars' worth of gas, which was enough for the trip at the time. Uncle Elmer disagreed and put five dollars' worth into the car and then asked Jerry if he needed more. Jerry said no and explained that he'd try to pay for the gas tomorrow or the next day when he collected some money. Uncle Elmer replied, "You're not paying me until you've got the money to pay. If you never pay me, I'm happy seeing you work. Go and do the Lord's work!" With God's blessing and Uncle Elmer's generosity, Jerry and Dennis were able to visit a young girl facing serious surgery.

Jerry and Dennis made the trip to Children's Hospital in Birmingham and went in to see Rhonda Taylor. They began to talk to her and to place her at ease with their visit. Jerry was armed with his Soul Winning New Testament containing the book of Psalms that he always carried with him as he visited and ministered. Rhonda explained that she was a member of Sardis Baptist Church, but that she only attended church sometimes when she spent the night with a friend. During their conversation, Jerry—sensing that everything was not right with her life—asked her if she was saved. She replied, "I don't know what you are talking about." They talked about the surgery she was facing, the amputation of her leg at the knee, because of bone cancer.

Jerry then said, "Would you like for me to have prayer with you and then you ask God to save you?"

She replied, "Yes."

Jerry explained what being saved meant and how people could be saved by confessing their sins and inviting Jesus into their lives, thereby being born again, becoming a member of God's family, and being a joint heir with Jesus Christ, who would strengthen and uphold them. They then prayed together, asking God to hear her prayer and come into her life. At the conclusion of the prayer, Rhonda exclaimed, "Everything is brighter, everything is lighter!"

Jerry asked, "What has happened?"

She replied, "God told me He had saved me!"

During the visit, she had noticed the annotated and highlighted New Testament that Jerry was carrying and asked if she could see it. She then asked Jerry if she could borrow it. He gladly replied, "No, you can't borrow it, but you can have it to keep." With that, he presented the testament to the girl. She was very happy to receive her very own testament and then, after placing the testament on her chest, expressed her sincere thanks to Jerry for the gift.

The next day, the day of the operation, the surgeon came to visit the young lady beforehand. She showed the testament to him and said, "You are going to operate on my left leg today. Would it hurt anything if I leave this here during the operation? My preacher came to see me last night and I got saved. He gave me this."

The surgeon replied, "No, but there is one thing I'd like to say. I won't touch you unless you let me have prayer with you before I operate." With that being said, the surgeon bowed by the bed and had prayer with her. Although the surgeon did his best with God's help, complications arose during the surgery, originally set to remove the left leg at the knee, which required the entire leg be removed at the hip joint.

The visit with the girl facing surgery became a multi-faceted blessing to several people. Jerry trusted God for help to get to Birmingham and received more than he asked for; Uncle Elmer got a blessing in providing a way for God's work to be done; Jerry and Dennis got to minister to a young girl who had a great need; and that young girl facing serious surgery received Christ into her life and was gloriously saved. What a lesson this situation was! A simple hospital visit conducted by God's leadership turned into a chain reaction of events that led to people being saved and the improvement of relationships in the church.

God then began a profound work in Butler Baptist Church after Rhonda Taylor's surgery. During and after recovery, she led her mother back into the church. She then led her unsaved stepfather to Christ and followed that action by leading her stepfather's brother to Christ. God blessed her efforts in a mighty way after she gave her life unto Him and until He called her home about two years later. She was instrumental in helping turn the church around after Jerry Ross and Dennis Oliver witnessed to her during a visit to her bedside and succeeded in their efforts to lead her to Christ. Everyone who had a part in this touching experience gave God the glory for the outcome.

Rhonda's mother Nell had been out of the church for years after the church had withdrawn its fellowship from her. Rhonda's witnessing and exuberance for serving Christ led Nell to come back to the church, confess her wayward lifestyle and its many sins, apologize to the church, and ask its forgiveness. She and her husband came to the altar and prayed through as they both agonized with God. Nell made things right with the Lord, and her husband Donnie was saved. Upon getting her life back in order with God, Nell arose from the altar, faced the church, and said, "God has forgiven me, but I know that you may not be able to forgive me after the things I've done. But, if there's any way in your heart you can forgive me, please forgive me."

Jerry said that it was a beautiful and earnest confession and plea for forgiveness straight from the heart of a truly repentant person. Dennis Oliver was so impressed by the sincerity of Nell's statement and request that he quickly arose and said, "Brother moderator, I make a move that we totally reinstate this lady to the fellowship that we withdrew from her so many years ago, and that we reinstate her to full rights and fellowship of the church." When Nell's husband Donnie heard Brother Dennis's move, he said, "Can you take me in now, too?"

Dennis replied, "Yes, but you'll come as a candidate for baptism and after baptism, to full rights and fellowship of the church."

After Donnie was accepted, contingent upon his baptism, Rhonda came forward and petitioned the church for membership and as a candidate for baptism. She was wearing a full prosthesis at the time but was experiencing a great deal of difficulty with its use. Consequently, she later stopped using the artificial leg and made out without it. After joining the church, she continued her dedicated and highly committed work for the church. Jerry was amazed at how quickly she could make her way to the altar for invitations calls and other special prayer times. Although she had only one leg, she would many times beat other people to the altar. She had a great desire to pray for sinners and all those with special needs who came for prayer. During the remainder of her short life, Rhonda Taylor was an inspiration to Jerry and the membership of Butler Baptist Church. She was a stalwart warrior in God's army here on this earth, but He saw fit to call her home to heaven and her new body in a few months The crowds of family, friends, and loved ones attending her funeral service overflowed the church and were a tremendous testament of their love and appreciation for her. During her life, she made a difference for God and His work, and her works for Him will be long remembered.

God continued to bless Butler Baptist Church, and the growth pattern that it had begun to experience at the time continued. That growth was not without problems, however, and Pastor Jerry Ross was sorely tested as he dealt with those problems and sought amiable solutions for them. His first pastorate, Butler Baptist, was a veritable on-the-job training experience for him as he began his ministry in God's field. Two of the important lessons he learned early in that ministry were that he must always seek God's leadership and that he must always depend on and trust wholeheartedly in that leadership in all things and then put that leadership to use.

As time went by, Jerry had to deal with a couple of social issues within the church. In one of them, a person was offended because of a proposed action by the church. He met the problem head-on and dealt with it forthrightly. It became evident to him at the time that there are occasions when it is necessary to stand up for the rights of the church and to defend the interests of its members as long as they are in accordance with the will and principles of God.

As Jerry expanded his program of visitation in the community, the expansive needs for visitation within the area and in the name of the church demanded that he put full-time effort to the program. He did not have time to work the job that provided his livelihood and to do the work of his calling at the same time. Depending on God to supply his needs, he gave up his job in order to allow time for God's work and to pursue his goals of field ministry and growth of the church.

It was during this time that he experienced one of the most challenging situations of his ministry to date. As Jerry was gaining experience and knowledge about his pastorate, Butler Baptist, he had sought to pay visits to all the active church members as well as to those members who had become inactive for some unknown reason. He learned about a situation in which a former member had withdrawn from the church because of some dispute within the church. Armed with only limited knowledge about the problem, Jerry set out to rectify the situation, with the goal of getting all of the parties involved back into church. His first step was to visit the aggrieved man and his family, in a preliminary attempt to learn the source of the problem and then develop a plan to resolve it.

During his visitation work in the community, Jerry, accompanied by his friend Dennis Oliver, went to the home of the former member of Butler Baptist Church, who was an older man with a fairly large family, and introduced himself. He felt that in order to deal with a person's problems, the first thing you had to do was to gain that person's confidence. Jerry tried to do everything he could to do just that, perhaps placing too much emphasis on his own ability to deal with the problem. After the initial greetings and formalities had been completed, he resorted to some congenial, lighthearted small talk as an icebreaker for what was to follow. As Jerry and his host were visiting, a young woman came through the room where they were. Jerry, making an assumption about the relationship of the young woman, got off on the wrong foot when he inquired if she was one of the man's daughters. The man replied very sternly and emphatically, "No, that's my wife!" As Jerry was regaining his aplomb and getting over his embarrassment, a pretty young girl of about six or seven years of age came into the room. As he was turning thoughts over in his mind that this young lady must be the man's granddaughter, Brother Dennis Oliver knew what he was thinking and then began to shake his head negatively. Finally, Jerry recovered and remarked to the man, "Now, that's a pretty little girl."

The man said, "Yes, that's my baby girl." Jerry heaved a sigh of relief after avoiding another embarrassing situation and moved on to other things. He looked in amazement at the age differences so evident in the members of the family. The wife was in her early thirties and her husband appeared to be approaching his seventies, and their youngest child was seven years old.

With that and a little more polite conversation about the church and the community, Jerry and Dennis left that residence with a burden for the situation that existed. Jerry had learned a valuable lesson from the visit, namely that it was expedient for a pastor to have a good working knowledge of the makeup of the families he was working with in the area of his pastorate.

As time went by and as he was led by the Lord, Jerry briefly visited the man on one or two occasions, but he did not make any progress whatsoever in getting the man and his family back into church. He was received less than cordially by the man as he told Jerry in forthright terms that he shouldn't make any more visits to his home. He emphasized in his remarks that Jerry was not welcome there. Although God continued to direct Jerry to go back to the man's home in an effort to win the man and his family back into the church, he was very reluctant to go because of the man's temperament, size, and total opposition to invitations to come back to church.

77

Jerry stayed away from that home for more than a month, but he did continue his visiting program in the community. While he was achieving some success in his efforts to increase the membership and attendance of Butler Baptist Church, God was still working with Jerry as he kept directing him to visit the disgruntled man and his family. He still carried a burden for the family, but he resisted the Master's directions to visit them while coming up with a number of excuses for not doing so. Eventually, however, Jerry did make another visit to the man's home.

Upon his arrival at the man's residence, Jerry was met with the usual cold treatment. Immediately, the man met Jerry with some harsh words when he said, "Now, I know where the church is; I know who you are and you told me your name's in the phone book. If I need you, I'll call you. You don't need to be coming back down here on me anymore."

Jerry responded, "Well, I understand what you are telling me, but as long as the Lord is leading me, I am coming."

In reply, the man said, "Well, I'm telling you that He ain't leading you, and you ain't coming back down here." Feeling a good bit of consternation about the situation, Jerry left once again.

About a month later, Jerry was visiting in the Butler Church area and felt a strong directive from God to visit the man again. Jerry had just begun working with an insurance company, and the job allowed him some amount of freedom from work during daytime hours. That day was such a day and he used the time to visit the man again. Upon his arrival at the home, the man's wife told Jerry that the man was out tending to his hogs a short distance from the house. She also explained that her husband was not in the best of moods at the time and that he was like an old hornet that particular day. She also advised that if Jerry wanted to go ahead and visit him, he should think seriously about it before doing so and then use his own best judgment if he decided to proceed with the visit. After considering what he knew God wanted him to do, Jerry chose to visit with the man.

The man, upon seeing Jerry, immediately went on the offense in a very determined way by saying, "I don't know what it is going to take to make you understand 'don't come back.' Leave, I don't want to listen to anything you've got to say. I don't like the church and I don't like the people of the church, and I don't like you."

Hearing those powerful words, Jerry moved back a safe distance from the man and said, "I want to have prayer." After receiving a very hard look from the man, he went ahead and offered a prayer on behalf of the situation. Jerry invoked God's blessing for the man and his family and asked for special help for the man that he could get things right and get back in church. Finally, he asked God to chastise the man if it was needed.

When Jerry concluded with his prayer, the man said, "Boy, if I see you again, I'm going to whip you!" Jerry knew the man was saying what he thought and that he would try to make good his promise. With that, Jerry took leave of the man and went on his way, still troubled about what was going on.

A short time later, Butler Baptist Church began a revival with the Reverend Johnny Camp as the evangelist for the services. One night during the revival, the service had just started, with Brother Dennis Oliver directing the congregation in a hymn. Jerry and Brother Camp were seated at the front of the church. Jerry happened to look up and saw the man he had been visiting and several members of his family coming through the door. The man, over six feet tall and very muscular, weighed nearly three hundred pounds and was a very imposing sight. Jerry pointed out the man to Brother Camp and said, "Brother Johnny, we've got trouble." Brother Camp inquired what it was and Jerry answered, "He said that the next time he saw me, he was going to whip me." Jerry explained about the early visits and a couple of return visits and the apparent failure his attempts to win the man and his family. All the while, the man was moving toward the front of the church with a stern look on his face and in his eyes.

Brother Dennis, the song leader, froze when he saw what was happening because Jerry had told him of the developments in the case, especially about the threat to whip Jerry the next time he saw him. The man reached the front of the church, and just as Jerry thought he was ready to step onto the stage and make good his promise, the man knelt in the altar and began to pray. He poured out his heart to God and asked for forgiveness. When he had finished praying, he made acknowledgments to the church and asked to be considered for membership once again. Jerry learned at that time that the church had withdrawn fellowship from him after his wife had died and he had married a much younger woman. That action had created problems that had festered over the years, but they were all solved that night during the service. The church restored the man's membership and granted him the full fellowship and rights of the church. As a result, the man and his family began to attend church once again and became fruitful members of the congregation. Over the next few months, nine members of the man's family were saved, baptized, and added to the church family. Jerry Ross gives God all the praise for that happy and glorious turnaround in a family's life. That was another time in his life that something wonderful had happened to him that was only through grace.

There was another very touching situation that occurred about a year into Jerry's ministry at Butler Baptist Church. During the visitation program being conducted at Butler Baptist, Jerry learned of an elderly man—respectfully known to everyone as Uncle George—who had become concerned about the condition of his soul. Brother Jerry and several others made a number of visits to Uncle George, assisted him in needed ways and helped him to pray through and make a great change in his life.

God's blessings had been showered on Butler Baptist Church in a mighty way, and the blessings continued to come as people obeyed His will. Pastor Jerry and some other members of the church continued the visitation program and expanded upon it. They were going door-to-door in a humble and low-key manner as they carried the Good News of Jesus Christ to the community. Jerry and some of the other members were getting such joy out of the visitation program that they visited several nights a week for the sole purpose of telling community members the story of Jesus. The friendly and concerned manner in which they visited in the Butler Church area quickly helped them gain the respect of the community, and as a result, they were accepted into the community. Because of God's blessing and their sincere and tireless efforts, the church began to grow and exhibit a newfound closeness of the membership that had been missing in the immediate past.

Pastor Jerry Ross, always looking for ways to help the cause, made a proposal to the church that he thought might increase attendance. He told the membership that he would sing a solo special on the appointed Sunday morning if they could get 100 people in Sunday school on that day. Although attendance had gotten noticeably better, it was still well below 100 people. In view of that, he felt that his members could never reach the goal and he would be safe from having to sing a solo. Now, Jerry was definitely not known for his singing ability and had never sung a solo. He definitely is not a Frank Sinatra or Jack Toney when it comes to singing. In fact, some have said without any reservation that he could not carry a tune in a bucket and that his voice sounded somewhat like a rock crusher grinding some particularly hard and tough rocks. He is an excellent preacher, but the same cannot be said for his singing. The appointed day arrived and a large crowd of people showed up for Sunday school. The count from the classes revealed that 120 people were on hand for Sunday school that day. Jerry Ross responded according to the deal he had made with the congregation and delivered his solo, which was somewhat less than a classic rendition. For some reason, the congregation did not ask him to sing again, nor would they make any more deals that required Jerry to sing. The Bible does indicate that we are to make a "joyful noise unto the Lord," but Jerry's singing may go beyond a joyful noise. For a fact, the Butler Baptist Church congregation accepted a good-natured challenge issued by the dedicated pastor, Jerry Ross, and then enjoyed working toward a goal and exceeding it by 20 percent. God had blessed once again with that humorous incident, and He was glorified in it all by Pastor Jerry Ross and the congregation of Butler Baptist Church. He was using unusual situations to test a beginning pastor, to expand a congregation and draw it together, and to bring glory to His name.

Another interesting situation developed at Butler Baptist that tested Pastor Ross and Brother Donnie Hudgins, a member of the church. A beekeeper in the community, Mr. Reagan, had several hives of honeybees that he had developed and maintained for several years. He was an experienced beekeeper who very carefully looked after his bees. He looked forward to harvesting the fruit of his labors as he thought about the golden delicacy being prepared and stored by the bees. His hives were equipped with extra square boxes, called supers, for the bees to fill with honey in the honey-making season. The top supers were reserved for Mr. Reagan to remove for his own use and enjoyment. The honey in the lower section of the hive was left for the bees to use for food through the winter months and at other times as they needed it. Mr. Reagan had been stricken with mouth cancer and was unable to tend to his bees and collect the honey that year.

Jerry and Donnie Hudgins went by to visit Mr. Reagan one day as they were out visiting in the community. After visiting for a while and having prayer with the Reagans, they asked Mr. Reagan if there was anything they could do for him. He said, "No, boys, there is nothing I need at the time, but there is one thing that needs to be done. My bees need to be checked. I am sick and am not able to check on them or do anything for them. I do know that the hives are full of honey and I am afraid they'll start leaking and cause insects and worms to invade the hives and destroy my bees. Could you boys check the hives and harvest the honey for me?"

Jerry and Donnie looked at each other in amazement as they heard the request. They prayed silently, asking for God's help in dealing with the request at hand. With His blessing and assurance, they set a time and decided to tackle the job of robbing bees for the very first time in their lives.

They asked Mr. Reagan many questions about the task at hand: What equipment is needed? How do you keep the bees from stinging? Are there special clothes? What are the steps of the harvesting process? Fortunately, Mr. Reagan had all the answers and the required equipment, and the two first-time honey harvesters set about their job. Their wives and Mrs. Reagan were in the kitchen, awaiting the outcome of Jerry and Donnie versus the bees.

Prior to approaching the bees, Jerry and Donnie had prayer, asking God's help for themselves as they tried to render the help needed by Mr. Reagan. They then put on the heavy clothing, the bee bonnets, and the gloves, and tied off their pants cuffs to prevent the bees from getting into their pants. They stuffed the cloth rags in the smoker, lit it, and set about the task at hand. By following Mr. Reagan's instructions explicitly and plying the smoker excessively, they were able to remove the full frames of honey from the hives and carry them to the house for their wives and Mrs. Reagan to process. While processing the honey and packing it in jars, each of the ladies received several stings. It seems that a number of the bees had come into the house with the honey and succeeded in making their presence known to the ladies in a forthright and painful manner. The wives accepted their fate good-naturedly, but were perturbed by the fact that neither Jerry nor Donnie received a single sting. They were reluctant, however, to let the men forget that they had endured the stings while they worked with the honey in the house. Jerry and Donnie good-naturedly suggested that perhaps the women's faith was not as strong as theirs. Brother Jerry and Donnie felt that God had given them a special blessing as they obeyed His guidance and helped a man who needed help in doing something he could not do for himself. The bee-robbing episode by Jerry and Donnie was the subject of conversation at Butler Baptist in the ensuing days. There was a great deal of wonder and admiration directed at the two of them as a result of their successful efforts in completing the task. Perhaps some of the members wondered if they would do it again if God directed them to do it. Brother Jerry and Brother Donnie say to this day that they would do His bidding if He directed them, but as of this day, "He hasn't and they haven't."

There was a great lesson in the honey-harvesting situation. God can use a willing person, regardless of his inexperience or lack of skills, and give him all that is needed to perform a seemingly impossible job if that person is willing to fully trust and follow God's leadership. Once again, God had brought Jerry Ross through a scary situation and made it a graphic example of what His love and grace can do for a trusting and committed Christian as he works in God's field.

God had blessed Butler Baptist Church in so many ways and in so many situations. Brother Jerry and the growing membership of Butler Baptist stood in awe of what God was accomplishing in their midst. God took almost unreal things in Jerry's life and made something out of them. Those things became beneficial elements in what God was doing in Butler Church and, indeed, what God was doing for Reverend Jerry Ross and his individual ministry. God had led Jerry Ross to spend a great deal of his pastoral time visiting in the church community, witnessing, and telling the Good News of Jesus Christ and inviting members of the community to come to Butler Baptist. Now He was giving Jerry some very valuable on-the-job training by placing him in a variety of situations that required Jerry to seek God's leadership and depend totally on Him for the strength and knowledge to complete the task assigned to him by God.

Jerry continued his ministry at Butler Baptist for three years, and God continued to bless him and the church in a mighty way. After three years, however, Jerry received a call to be the pastor of Rehoboth Baptist Church in Guntersville, Alabama. God led Jerry to accept the call to Rehoboth. Jerry loved Butler Church and would have liked to remain there for a long time, but he accepted God's will and the call to Rehoboth. With a great deal of sadness, He resigned as pastor of Butler Baptist Church and said goodbye to his friends and the work there, and then moved on to Rehoboth Baptist Church and a new work in Guntersville.

Rehoboth Baptist Church was different from Brother Jerry's previous pastorate at Butler Baptist Church. While the basic doctrines and affiliations of each church were basically the same, there were notable differences between the two groups. The people of the Guntersville church differed from typical Sand Mountain Churches in their style of worship and in the expression of their feelings. Some of their beliefs and ideals were expressed differently and their dedication and commitment took a different path to fulfillment. Their worship was genuine and sincere, but was practiced in a manner that was different from that which Jerry had been accustomed to on Sand Mountain.

Soon after arriving at Rehoboth, Brother Jerry learned that the church had recently split. The former pastor and about sixty of the members had left Rehoboth as a result of the split. Jerry did not know him or the departed members. After he had been at Rehoboth for a short time, he became concerned about the situation and its effect on the church. One time, in the quietness of the midnight hour, Jerry awoke with the departed pastor on his mind. He was burdened with an overwhelming desire to learn something about that former pastor. Early the next morning, he called one of the deacons in an effort to fill in the blanks about the split and the contribution of the former pastor. The deacon was an older man and a solid, experienced Christian and deacon. He was very knowledgeable about the circumstances surrounding the split and the former pastor. He counseled Jerry about the situation and said, "Son, you don't know it, but he has been going all over the country talking about you and trying to get them to throw you out. So you need to prepare yourself. He's got sixty members." With that advice, Jerry directed his attention to restoring peace and harmony in Rehoboth.

Shortly after arriving there, Jerry began a program of visitation for Rehoboth Baptist. Some of the members joined him in carrying out the program. One of the areas they began to visit was a trailer park located a short distance away from the church. Some of the members and friends of the church advised against visiting there, citing drug problems, alcoholism, and resident rowdies as the reason for their advice. Jerry was undaunted by the negativism toward the visitation program and plunged into the program with renewed vigor. He said, "Praise the Lord! That's what God wants us to do: visit the sinners." With that, he and several of the members pushed ahead with the program. They were rewarded for their efforts.

Slowly, the visitation program began to pay dividends as several of the residents of the trailer park began to attend church; a few of them were saved and joined the church. The church began to experience slow but consistent growth as the work continued.

During that time, the Thanksgiving season was over and the Christmas season was rapidly approaching. Jerry had been counting his blessings, and in doing so, found that he and his wife Darlene had been abundantly blessed. They had a fine young son, Daryl, who was the pride of the entire family and the only grandchild on Darlene's side of the family and the youngest grandson on Jerry's side. They had all the necessities of life in ample measure and God was blessing Jerry's ministry in a mighty way. Furthermore, Daryl's grandparents, parents, and other family members had showered him with toys, fruits, candy, and everything else a young boy could possibly want. With all of this on his mind and with thankfulness in his heart for so many blessings, Jerry went to the weekly visitation night at Rehoboth.

While they were planning the visitation for that Tuesday night, one of the deacons offered a suggestion about where some of them should go that night. He said to Jerry, "Preacher, I have been praying all day, and if you haven't got someone really burning on your heart, I do have a family that has been burning on mine all day. The family is composed of a man and his wife and their young son. The little boy is about the age of yours. We need to visit them."

Jerry, having no plans of his own, said, "Yes, let's go to see them." With that, Jerry and the deacon and a couple of other men got into the car and set out to visit that family.

The family lived north of the Tennessee River and on the east side of Highway 431. They lived down a rough and unpaved country road some distance from the highway. Their home was an old Airstream travel trailer. When Jerry and his party arrived at the home, the couple immediately invited them in and seemed very pleased to have visitors come into their humble home. The home had no television set or other conveniences, and the stove oven was open and being used for heat. There was no food in evidence in the sparsely furnished home. The baby was very unkempt and its diapers had been made from pieces of cloth torn from a yellow bed sheet that had been set aside for that purpose. The father was crippled by a withered hand, and both of them were slightly challenged in other ways.

Despite their problems, they were a friendly and appreciative couple who were glad to have visitors, but it appeared to Jerry and those with him that the couple had been placed in that location for a purpose.

After a brief visit with the couple and viewing the squalid conditions in which they were living, Brother Jerry and his friends from Rehoboth returned to the church. Jerry was so touched by what he had seen that he cried all the way back to the church. Once they were back at the church, they had a special prayer for the deserving couple they had just visited. After the prayer, they talked about what they could do to help the family. Since Christmas was upon them, the men knew they could use some money. Jerry spoke first and said, "Men, I haven't got much money, but would one of you take what I've got back to that family?" With that, he emptied his wallet to help the cause.

Right away, another of the men said, "Yes, and take what I've got, too." He gave everything he had in his pocket to the worthy cause. Deacon Riddle volunteered to take the money to the family and also contributed what he had to the cause.

Deacon Riddle carried the money to the couple that same night and gave them some sound, fatherly advice on how to spend it wisely. He advised them to buy propane gas for the home heating system, gasoline for their car, and the much-needed food. He also advised them about personal hygiene in a fatherly way. Finally, he invited them to church on Sunday. The ladies of the church, upon learning of the family's needs, collected clothing for all the family and other personal items for all members of the family and got them delivered to the home. Jerry's wife Darlene shared some of their young son's clothing with the family.

The congregation of Rehoboth Baptist Church was very happy to see the family come to church the next Sunday. The members of the church welcomed the family with open arms and did their best to make them feel loved and wanted. The members of the church were very happy that God had called for the church to something for a downtrodden but deserving family. The visiting family was the very picture of happiness and appreciation because of the wonderful things that had been done for them. They reciprocated by showing love and sincere appreciation to the church. Whenever the family came to church, there would be hugs all around for the man and his wife and lots of genuine attention to the baby. All the attention and good things from the church overwhelmed the couple.

Whereas they had been neglected in the past, they were now the center of attention for the membership of Rehoboth Church.

There was a lesson in that situation for Jerry. Christmas was just around the corner at the time the situation occurred. Christmas was normally a quiet time for the Ross family, a time when they exchanged simple gifts, enjoyed a good family get-together, and observed the true meaning of Christmas. While Jerry and his family were looking forward to a good Christmas, it was obvious that the needy family was facing a very bleak Christmas. When he compared what the destitute family had before the church intervened with what he had been blessed with at his home, he realized just how fortunate he had been and the tremendous extent of his blessings. He realized that he and his family probably wasted and discarded more food than the unfortunate couple had to eat on a given day. Beyond that, Daryl had a great amount of toys all through the house; so many, in fact, that Jerry often grumbled about having to step over them. Jerry, Darlene, and Daryl also had a very comfortable home, as well as good health. As Jerry thought about all those things, he was overwhelmed with gratitude to God for all He had done for the Ross family. He was doubly glad that God had given him and the church the opportunity help a family that desperately needed help. The unbounded joy, happiness, and thankfulness exhibited by the needy couple upon receiving the help was a great blessing to Jerry and the congregation. The overall result of the situation taught Jerry a lesson good for a lifetime.

One of the highlights of Jerry's ministry at Rehoboth occurred on February 14 of that year. On that date and in the middle of the winter, a number of those new converts asked for baptism. To Jerry's surprise, the candidates for baptism asked to be baptized in Guntersville Lake. They looked on baptisteries with considerable disdain. Besides that, they had a beautiful place on the lakeshore that was excellent for baptizing. Not only did they want to be baptized in the lake, they wanted to be baptized immediately, regardless of the fact that it was midwinter. This request was a severe test of Jerry's faith, and he had quite a struggle in maintaining it at the time. He did agree to go ahead with the service if the candidates wanted it that way. They did indeed want it that way. The fact that Jerry had always been very susceptible to catching cold didn't help his feeling at all. He recalled previous experiences in doing God's work and remembered that He had always supplied his needs. Jerry began to pray and to lay his need before God. He told God that he had made a promise to do the baptism without thinking it through, and now he needed His help. Jerry was not trying to force God to do anything; rather, he was letting Him know that he fully trusted in Him and was sincerely asking for His help. Peace came over Jerry about his upcoming baptismal service, to the extent that he was looking forward to it, even hoping that none of the candidates backed out of the service.

The day of the baptismal service arrived and the time came to enter the icy waters of the lake on that cold February afternoon. Jerry and the candidates joined hands and formed a line as they went into the water. As he got into waist-deep water, Jerry was so cold he thought he would freeze. Once again, he beseeched God for His help. He said, "Lord, this is all for You and in Your honor and for Your glory, and I have got to have Your help." Jerry said the response was immediate and was like a switch had been flipped. He was not cold anymore. He asked the candidates how they were and they replied that they were in fine shape. He went ahead with the service and baptized all the candidates, who ranged in age from eight years to fifty-six years. All of the candidates remained in the water until the service was complete, and then they and Jerry exited the water together. They went to the nearby homes of some of the members to change clothes to prepare for the night's service. The baptismal service was completed that night at the church as the newly baptized candidates received the right hand of Christian and church fellowship from the church members. An additional blessing of God was that none of those baptized or Pastor Jerry Ross got the slightest hint of a cold from their icy encounter with the waters of Guntersville Lake on that chilly February day.

A week later, all the newly baptized church members and the pastor were still completely free of cold symptoms.

God continued to bless Rehoboth Baptist Church in a mighty way. Before the year was out, Jerry was blessed to see fifty-odd people come back to the church and rejoin the fellowship of Rehoboth. A considerable number of them requested baptism into the fold. With God's great help and divine leadership, Jerry and the congregation of Rehoboth were able to achieve many successes in the Lord's work. Although Jerry's first year of service as pastor of Rehoboth Baptist Church was a successful year for him and the congregation, he quickly gives God complete credit and glory for the things that were achieved there during that year. He is quick to point out that it is nothing he has done of himself, but it is what God has done through a faithful, believing, and available servant.

Rehoboth Baptist Church was different from most other Southern Baptist churches, in that it called pastors on a yearly basis. Jerry was aware of this from the time he had come to Rehoboth as pastor. As the church year was drawing to an end and the time for the election of a pastor for the coming year was fast approaching, Jerry began to think about the church and what had been accomplished in his year as pastor at Rehoboth. He could count a number of good things that God had provided for the church throughout the year, but there was a foreboding in his heart and mind concerning the church and what it faced in the new church year. God had revealed to Jerry that problems were ahead for the church and its members. Although a great deal of progress had been made in restoring the church, there were still issues that clouded the future of Rehoboth. Jerry began to have feelings that maybe he should not allow his name to be placed in consideration for pastor during the coming church year. He was concerned about those new converts whom he had been instrumental in leading to Christ, and he did not want to do anything that would hurt them. He prayed for God's leadership and guidance as he made his decision about whether or not to offer himself as a candidate for pastor of Rehoboth for the coming year. After Jerry had spent much time in prayer and agonizing over the issue, God gave him the liberty to refuse the request if he was asked to be a candidate for pastor. Brother Jerry felt that his work at Rehoboth was nearing completion and that he should refuse any invitation to be a candidate for pastor. God confirmed Jerry's feelings and Jerry made his decision known to the Deacon Board.

In a called meeting, he told the members of the Deacon Board about his decision. He said, "The Lord has given me liberty that I can leave. I have prayed a lot about it and I am going to leave with no intention of going anywhere else to another church or any other such thing. You have taught me a good lesson." Jerry was a bit discouraged about the prospect of facing a pastor election and the possibility of facing an opponent for the position every year.

The Deacon Board countered with the statement, "Yes, we are going to nominate you for pastor for the coming year."

Jerry once again stated his position, "Do not recommend me for pastor. I won't accept it. I will not accept the position even if I get 100 percent of the vote. The Lord has relieved me and given me liberty to leave Rehoboth."

The Deacon Board went ahead with their plan and held an election for pastor that pitted Jerry against an opponent. The opponent, who was pastor immediately prior to Jerry, won the election by about ten votes and accepted the call of Rehoboth Church to be its pastor. The Deacon Board contacted Jerry and told him the opponent had won. Jerry sternly responded, "I told you not to run me as a candidate for pastor. I asked some people not to vote for me if I was nominated. They would have voted me in if I had let them go." The Deacon Board allowed that that was the way they had always done it.

Following the election, Jerry officially resigned as pastor of Rehoboth Baptist Church. He felt comfortable with the action he had taken. He was satisfied with the results of his ministry at Rehoboth and left with a feeling that he had completed the work God had given him to do. At the time, God had given Jerry no burden or calling to pastor another church, but he was willing and ready to do God's will, should He have more work for him to do in the future.

Shortly thereafter, Jerry received a call from a Mr. Mickey Swords of Albertville, Alabama. Mr. Swords cut directly to the issue when he said, "You don't know me and we've never met, but I'm from Corinth Baptist Church that is located on Water Line Road in the Albertville area."

Jerry remarked, "That's the church where Bobby Bright used to pastor. I've visited that church during revival."

Mr. Swords explained the reason for his call. He stated that Corinth was without a pastor at the time, and then he asked Jerry if he would come and preach for them. Jerry agreed to come and fill an appointment, but he explained that he didn't feel the Lord's leadership for pastoral work at the time. Mr. Swords extended the invitation once again and asked Jerry to pray about accepting the invitation. He pointed out that the congregation wanted to hear him and that the pulpit committee would be listening at the same time.

Jerry accepted the invitation and went to Corinth Baptist to preach on the appointed day. At the completion of the service, Jerry was left with an empty feeling and a painful thought that he had been a failure on that day. He felt that he had not accomplished anything for God's cause that day. Before he left Corinth that day, he did talk to some of the deacons, however, and told them that he was "burned out." He related some of the situations he had encountered in the past year and some of the less-than-cordial treatment he had received. Jerry then explained that he didn't feel that he should take another church at the time. He was concerned that he might not do a good job. The group at Corinth was still interested and told Jerry to go home and pray about it. He stated that he would do that.

Jerry did what he promised he would do: he prayed earnestly about what God would have him do in the pastoral field. The group at Corinth called him in about two weeks and asked him if he would come and preach for them again. Jerry said, "Yes, I will." An appointment was made and Jerry went back to Corinth and preached again. He delivered his message and returned home. He didn't hear from Corinth for about two weeks after filling his second appointment there.

Those two weeks turned out to be a painful time for Jerry. Many thoughts and doubts coursed through his mind, and he was filled with dread about his future as a minister of God's word. He couldn't sleep; he was nervous and worried; his food didn't taste right; and above all, he had a deep concern about where he stood with God. During that period, God revealed to Jerry that his problem was related to his rebelliousness toward God and his ministry at that time. God also revealed to Jerry that he had fulfilled his appointments at Corinth without fully trusting Him for guidance and leadership in a new venture. Once again, Jerry Ross received a repeat lesson in placing God first in all things and in seeking His counsel and leadership in all things. After all that, Jerry knew that he should prayerfully consider any call to serve that God might send his way.

A couple of weeks later, he was called to pastor Corinth Baptist Church. The call was a surprise to him because he felt that he had made a very poor showing both times he had preached at Corinth. He acted on faith and God's leadership as he accepted the call and went on the field in the Corinth community. The fact that the pastor at Corinth Baptist served as a bi-vocational pastor did not deter him from accepting the call, but Jerry knew deep inside that he would like to be a full-time pastor.

Seven or eight weeks after he accepted the call to Corinth Baptist, Jerry received a call from a church in the suburbs of Chicago, Illinois, asking him to come and preach for them. They were without a pastor at the time and were diligently seeking a minister to fill the position. The Reverend Raymond Cook, the longtime pastor of Antioch Baptist Church in Albertville, Alabama, had a connection with that church and had given them Jerry's name prior to Jerry's call to Corinth Baptist. Brother Cook had told Jerry a little information about the Chicago church and the fact that it required a full-time pastor prior to Jerry's Corinth call. For some time, Jerry had felt God's leadership to be a full-time pastor and was praying about and considering going to the Chicago church when Corinth Baptist called him to be pastor.

Jerry did contact the Chicago church and its search committee to learn more about their pastoral needs. They were insistent that he come and preach, and said that they would send plane tickets for him and his wife Darlene to come to Chicago for a weekend and preach for them. They set a time for the visit a couple of weekends in the future, and Jerry and Darlene began to make plans for the visit. Not wishing to keep anything from his congregation and in a move to keep them informed, he explained to the Deacon Board about what he planned to do. He thought that the opportunity to preach at the Chicago church might lead to the fulfillment of his dream of being a full-time pastor.

It is interesting to note that there had not been any moves seeking salvation, re-dedications, or help with other spiritual need in the weeks that Brother Jerry had been pastor of Corinth Baptist Church. Thoughts that he might have made a mistake in coming to Corinth coursed through his mind. The devil, in an attempt to derail Jerry's ministry, began to tell him that he had stepped out on his own and that the Lord was not with him anymore. Jerry had to do lots of praying and asking God for His help and direction on the direction his ministry should take.

God changed Jerry's plans in a mighty way the very next weekend, and at the same time, confirmed his call to Corinth again. On that particular weekend preceding the planned trip to Chicago, God blessed Pastor Jerry and the Corinth congregation in a marvelous way. There was a special feeling in Jerry's heart when he arrived at the church that Sunday and it caused him to do something before the service started that he had never done before. He had a compelling feeling to get God's message out in the community surrounding Corinth Baptist Church. Without hesitation and with the Spirit's leading, he went to the front door of the church, faced the community, and said in a loud voice, "Get saved! Get saved! Get

92

saved!" Even though he didn't completely understand what had happened, he knew that God had directed it.

Jerry described the service that followed as one of the sweetest services he had ever been in. One or two people were gloriously saved during that service, and the presence of the Holy Spirit filled the sanctuary. The Lord spoke to Jerry following the service and reminded him once again of what could and would happen when he depended on Him and followed His instruction and guidance. Jerry now knew for sure that his mission for God was to serve as pastor of Corinth Baptist Church.

That development left Jerry Ross with a piece of unfinished business. He still had the invitation to preach in Chicago, accompanied by the promise of plane tickets to Chicago for him and his wife. He called the church in Chicago and told them that he would still come and preach if they so desired, but he would not be a candidate for pastor of the church. He explained that even though he had a burning desire to be a full-time pastor, he knew that God wanted him to be at Corinth and that he shouldn't accept the expensive plane tickets to Chicago. The Deacon Board of the Chicago church understood Jerry's predicament and expressed as much in a conference call with him. They commended him for being up front with them and wished him well in his work at Corinth. They assured him that they had a contingency plan in place for pastor selection and that they were putting it into action at the time and were looking to the future with great anticipation and trust in the Lord. Thus began Reverend Jerry Ross's five-year ministry at the Corinth Baptist Church near Albertville, Alabama.

Corinth Baptist Church experienced a slow but steady growth from the beginning of Jerry Ross's ministry there. The membership as a whole was supportive of his work and plans for Corinth. Several family groups stepped forward as leaders of the programs at the church. Visitation was a key element in the growth of the church. Work with the youth of the church was another. A member of one of the highly respected families of the church announced his calling to preach during Jerry's tenure at Corinth Baptist and went on to a successful ministry of his own. There was a sweet spirit permeating the parishioners at Corinth as they all joined hands with Pastor Jerry Ross to follow the leadership and promptings of God. There were feelings of thankfulness and satisfaction as God began to reward their efforts. The church conference records attest to the many good things God brought to Corinth during the Ross years. Jerry and the membership give all the glory and praise to God for all the things He brought to fruition at Corinth.

An example of one of the unusual happenings that occurred during that period involved Jerry Ross and Milford Waldrop, one of the church members. They were attending a sale of equipment one weekend and were looking for items they could use for themselves. One of the items they saw was a used school bus. It was a nice bus and in excellent condition, complete with a new set of tires. Milford was the first to see it, and he found Jerry and said to him, "Preacher, we need to buy that bus for the church."

Jerry was aghast at first, but the more he looked at the bus and considered its possibilities, he said, "Well, whatever you want to do, we'll do it. We'll have to go to the bank and arrange for the money and then give them a check."

Milford replied, "We'll handle that. Don't you worry about that." Thus, Corinth Baptist Church became the owner of a bus without even knowing it at the time.

Jerry drove the bus to his shop at home, where he and some of his crew cleaned it up and painted it blue instead of traditional school bus yellow. They put the church name on the sides of the bus in large white letters. It was a sharp-looking and eye-catching bus for use in God's service. Milford and Jerry probably took some good-natured kidding about the bus and its loud color scheme. They were not deterred, however, in their quest to obtain a bus and put it to work in God's field. They prayed long and hard about how the bus could be used to promote God's work. They felt strongly that they should start a bus ministry at the church. Although they had bought the bus on their own and without authorization of the church conference, they presented their plan to the church.

While some of the older and more conservative members of the church were reluctant about buying the bus, the conference accepted and approved the request by majority vote. When one of the church members volunteered to take over the bus ministry immediately, that ministry was off and running at Corinth. The bus ministry that began with five or six children initially riding the bus was soon transporting larger loads of worshipers to Corinth Church. In addition to larger numbers of children, the passenger loads included many adults and older people. Milford and

Jerry were relieved that God had blessed their hasty action in buying the bus with remarkable results.

Although there was not an extensive youth program at Corinth, Jerry immediately saw that the bus would be a useful tool in working with the youth, and indeed, a way of leading them into a church relationship that would hopefully lead many of them to Christ. With that in mind, he met with some of the youth of the church and told them to be thinking about a trip that they would like to take. In the absence of a specific youth organization at Corinth, Brother Jerry later called the youth together and advised them to work together and come up with a chosen destination to visit as a group and then to start doing small projects to raise funds for the venture. He also told them to do their best to save some of their own for the selected trip. He stated that he would help them bring their plans and desires for a trip to fruition.

In about a month, the youth group came back to Brother Jerry and told him that they wanted to go to Six Flags over Georgia. Jerry hastily explained that such a trip would be expensive and that he might not have money for tickets and gas for the bus too. He called Six Flags and got ticket prices and reported back to the young people. Jerry wanted to help the group financially, but he was very surprised when they told him that they had the money for tickets and, beyond that, fifty dollars for gasoline for the bus. Happily, Brother Jerry said, "Let's go!"

On the appointed day, Brother Jerry and his wife and son, along with a couple of deacons and their wives, loaded a large group of young people on the blue-and-white bus and went to Six Flags. The group experienced a great day of fun and fellowship. Some of those church members who had also opposed the purchase of the bus were disturbed about the trip, thinking that modernism was creeping into the church. Thankfully, many of those same members later realized that the bus was being used efficiently in God's Kingdom work and then realized and acknowledged that they had been wrong about the program. They later stated their support for the bus ministry in a church service and became solid supporters of the program.

Jerry went on to serve Corinth as pastor for five years. God blessed his ministry there in many ways that are still fresh in his mind. Indeed, Jerry is cognizant of the blessings that God has bestowed on him from the battlefields of Viet Nam to the present time. As he considers them, he is overwhelmed with appreciation to the Loving God for the mercy and grace extended to him during all of those times. The old hymn, "Count Your Blessings," is especially meaningful to him and he is always moved with emotion as he tries to enumerate his blessings when he hears the song. He states that when he starts counting his blessings, he can't get past the one that occurred when he was saved. It was a glorious and life-changing experience as well as a powerful blessing for him, one that never fails to tug at his heartstrings. Although he is deeply grateful for the manifold blessings that God has bestowed on him throughout his life, he realizes that the plan of salvation is God's most precious gift to mankind. Throughout his ministry, Jerry has preached the good news of God's wonderful plan for the salvation of His creation, the fallen man. The chief goal of his ministry is and has always been to present the good news of God's loving gift to sinners and to warn them that the unconditional acceptance of that plan is absolutely essential if they are to reach heaven in the hereafter.

The work at Corinth was a work of faith and cooperation for the membership and Brother Jerry. Together they tackled several needs of the church. One of those needs was for a cemetery for the church. Corinth Baptist Church had not had a cemetery since the church was organized. The founding of a cemetery had been discussed by some of the members on some occasions in the past. Brother Jerry and several members of the church became serious about the establishment of a cemetery for Corinth and set out to bring the dream to fruition. The church was pleased to learn that the surrounding community was interested in the project and that an adjoining property owner was willing to sell the needed plot of land to the church at a fair price. The church borrowed five thousand dollars to purchase the five-acre parcel of land that adjoined the church property. When news of the project spread, the surrounding community became a willing participant in the project and began to support the actions with monetary contributions and donated work. As a result, the land purchase bank note was paid off in record time and Corinth Baptist Church became the owner of a needed cemetery.

The Cemetery Expansion Committee realized from the start of the project that the gravesites of the cemetery needed to be laid out properly to maximize the use of the land. They recommended that the new area be surveyed and platted by a professional surveyor. The committee wanted to

96

ensure that the platting provided the maximum number of gravesites as well as proper access to the sites. There are properly designed and placed driveways through the new cemetery to allow hearses to access all general areas of the cemetery. In addition to that, there are two-foot walkways interspersed throughout the whole area that allow easy access to any gravesite. Brother Jerry is particularly proud of that project, but he gives God all the credit for the good that was accomplished.

As Jerry's ministry at Corinth progressed, he and his wife Darlene enjoyed a familial relationship with the members of the church and grew to love the membership and its many families with a deep Christian love. Their fellowship with the congregation and the individual families was a profound blessing to Jerry and Darlene as they shared all the joys and sorrows of dedicated Christian service. In addition to many joyous occasions, there were times of sorrow that they experienced together.

One of those sorrowful times was when Brother Billy McCullars and his wife lost their beloved eighteen-month-old son in a freak accident. One Saturday afternoon, several boys were playing around the McCullarses' home. Being boys, they were seeking adventure by crawling under an electric fence that was "hot" at the time. Brother Billy's young son saw them going under the fence, apparently having fun, and he no doubt wanted to do the same thing. He began to crawl under the fence and, unfortunately, touched it. The current was coursing through the wire in short pulses, as it was set up to do by the controller. It is believed that the current pulsed at the same instant as the boy's heartbeat as he touched the wire. That event, when coupled with the fact that he was on moist ground, proved to be a fatal combination of events for the young child. The boy lost his life as a result of the current from the electric fence. He was rushed to the emergency room at the Boaz-Albertville Hospital, where all efforts to revive him failed. The doctor said that he had never seen anything that compared to that tragedy.

Understandably, the parents of the child, Billy and Betty McCullars, were very deeply grief-stricken and completely devastated over the sudden loss of their beloved young son. Billy blamed himself for the child's death, and he questioned God's part in the tragedy. He felt that God had been mean to him and let him down. He vowed to quit church and never go again, nor would he pray again. He even considered more serious consequences for himself. He was not receptive to counseling during that time.

Even though Brother Jerry and the church wanted to share the grief and help in any way possible, Brother Billy withdrew into himself and tried to bear his burden alone.

Brother Jerry decided that he and the others should give Brother Billy McCullars a little time to deal with his grief. They continued to pray for the family and made quiet offers of help, but they did not push anything on them. After a short time, Brother Jerry was led by God to visit the family to check on them and to see if anything was needed. Almost miraculously, Brother Jerry was led to invite Brother Billy to take a walk through the sixty-acre field of soybeans around Brother Billy's house. They had talked lightly about a few things, when God very plainly impressed Brother Jerry with some words to say to Brother Billy. Brother Jerry had learned that he must always listen to God and do his best to obey His instructions. He fully trusted and obeyed the leadership of God, and looked at Brother Billy and said, "Stop walking for a minute, Billy. The Lord has just shown me that your other son, Brock, is still alive. God also has just shown me that your other boy, had he lived, could have reached the age of sixteen years and then been killed in a terrible wreck when his car crashed into a tree. He would have died lost in that accident. As it is right now, he is in the hands of a just and loving God as an innocent little baby. He has got it much better than we have it today." Even though they had had prayer before leaving the house, Jerry asked that they have prayer again and ask God to give Billy and his family the strength and grace to get through the trying time. After the prayer, Brother Jerry said, "Billy, let's go to the house and get the dust and the dirt off of us. Do you remember the time David got out of the sackcloth and ashes after the tragedy in his life?"

Brother Billy replied, "I remember."

Jerry said, "Let's go back to the house and dust off spiritually and go back to serving God." Brother Billy heard those words in his heart and soul and never again mentioned harming or blaming himself; nor did he blame or curse God anymore. He went back to church and resumed his work for the Lord, and is doing so until this day. Brother Jerry praises God to this day for giving him the right words to say to a dear friend to help him understand God's love and the ever-present help He so freely offers in times of deep despair because of a tragic event.

Brother Jerry Ross's ministry at Corinth Baptist Church continued for just over five years and was filled with many joyous times and some sad times. Jerry and Darlene were truly blessed by the genuine fellowship they enjoyed with the congregation at Corinth as they all joined together in their service to God, the church, and the community. With their combined efforts and the generous leadership and help of God, Brother Jerry, Darlene, and the congregation were able to establish a steady growth pattern for Corinth Baptist that continued after Brother Jerry was called into other works. Among other things, the growth pattern later included a new church building.

Because of God's rich blessings and the wonderful Christian atmosphere at Corinth Baptist, leaving that ministry was not an easy thing for Jerry and Darlene Ross to accept and do. They loved the church and its people, and hated to leave this very satisfying work. In fact, Jerry sincerely said, "Leaving Corinth was one of the hardest things I ever had to do." Even so, he knew that he must follow God's leadership.

Jerry takes no credit at all for the success of his ministry at Corinth and at previous churches. He is quick to give all the credit to the Lord. In fact, he stands in amazement at the fact that God chose a vile and unlearned sinner with an eleventh-grade education to be one of His ministers. Realizing now how unlearned he really was and how little he knew about the Bible and God's work, Jerry loves to tell how God helped him to learn after he was saved and answered the call to preach the Word. He realized that his formal education was somewhat limited because he dropped out of school in the eleventh grade. Although he had been able to rely on his memory and make straight A's with very little studying through the seventh grade, his grades began a downward slide from then until he dropped out of school. After the call to preach came to Jerry, God then gave him a great thirst for knowledge about the Bible. He began to have marathon sessions of personal Bible study and prayer, with some of them lasting as long as four hours. With God's help and enlightenment, the Holy Bible, and Webster's Dictionary, Jerry was able to obtain a solid foundation for the demands of his new job as minister in God's field. This foundation was strengthened by learning experiences that came his way at each of the churches he served. He states that on-the-job training in God's field is some of the best training that a young minister can get.

Reverend Jerry Ross being honored on Pastor Appreciation Day at Pilgrim's Rest Baptist Church near Geraldine, Alabama

Reverend Jerry Ross delivering a sermon at Aurora Baptist Church during "Old Fashioned Day" services. He and the congregation dressed in period clothing that day.

A group of members of Aurora Baptist Church dressed in their period costumes on "Old Fashioned Day" services at the church.

Jerry Ross ready for church and proudly displaying a new jacket, a gift from Darlene.

Frontal View of Pilgrim's Rest Baptist Church at Geraldine, Al.

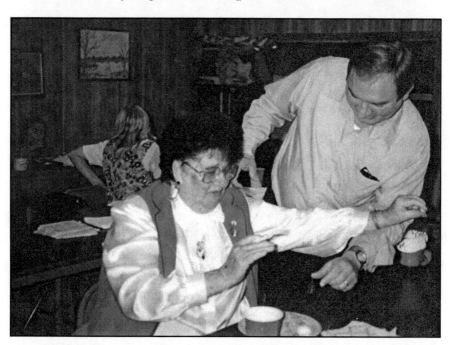

Brother Jerry pestering the Pilgrim's Rest Pianist, Bobbie Nell Gore, at a church social.

Reverend Jerry Ross, Darlene, Shane and Daryl at the time Jerry was completing his pastorate at Corinth Baptist Church.

Jerry and Darlene's son, Daryl, and other candidates for baptism entering Gilliland's pond for the baptismal service. Reverend Steve Young, the pastor of Jerry's home Church, is leading the candidates for baptism into the water.

Reverend Steve Young baptizing young Daryl Ross.

Reverend Jerry Ross charging the candidates for baptism, including his son, Daryl, prior to the baptism.

A recent photograph of Brother Jerry Ross and his family, circa 2004. Standing L to R - Avery, Cresap, Daryl, Shane, Dawn, Tyler. Seated L to R - Jerry, Darlene and Granddaughter Madisyn.

Reverend Jerry Ross and Dee Bagwell, a member of Pilgrim's Rest Baptist Church, while on a trip to the Smoky Mountains.

After completing his ministry at Corinth Baptist Church, Jerry returned to Butler Baptist Church for a period of a few months, basically on an interim basis. That short calling was followed by a call to East Lake Baptist Church in Guntersville, Alabama. Although Jerry resisted the call at first because of health problems and other hindrances, he later answered God's call to the East Lake church with enthusiasm and began his work there immediately after his call was approved by the church.

Jerry Ross had learned that each assignment God gave him was a unique situation and one that had its own set of rules, successes, challenges, and problems. To a large extent, the autonomy granted churches within the Southern Baptist Convention created those conditions. Early in his ministry, Jerry learned this solid fact of life and also learned that each new ministry was God's gift of on-the-job training for further ministries. Trusting and following God's leadership, he looked forward to the opportunity God was giving him at East Lake Baptist Church.

Serving at East Lake Baptist Church was a new experience for Jerry in a number of ways. First of all, his Christian philosophy was being broadened and deepened by God. He had been taught by God through personal study and meditation the real meaning of the cross. Many times, he had felt the need to stop what he was doing and ask for God's help in sorting out the elements of a particular situation he was facing at the time. Jerry felt a need for God's help in determining what his role was in a given situation. He knew he wasn't here because of justice or predestination. He knew he had not been born a Christian, but that there had been a very special requirement met when he became a Christian. The cross holding the Savior on Golgotha's hill became the very pinnacle of God's love for His most notable creation, mankind, as He bore the sins of the world on His shoulders as His blood was spilled for sinners. Since his acceptance of Christ and answering His call to preach, Jerry's ministry has always directed toward and centered upon the cross and the shed blood of Christ. That attitude was always basic in his ministry, regardless of which church he was serving at a given time. His emphasis has always firmly indicated that the only way sinners can come into a lasting and true relationship with Jesus Christ is to look to Him on the cross and accept that spilled blood that was freely shed for the sins of the world. Brother Jerry says that man must keep the scene of the cross before him at all times and that man must not be swayed by the winds of doubt created by the devil.

That simple message was, and is, the centerpiece of his message to a lost world. Jerry developed a firm philosophy about being a willing worker in God's field and seeking His guidance and then unerringly following His directions.

Secondly, going back to a city church in a different setting presented a new set of challenges to Jerry Ross. Simply put, a pastor coming into a new pastorate must be prepared to make a number of adjustments. Although with God's leadership he may bring new ideas to the table, he must be careful not to upset the established operational procedures of the church. While East Lake Baptist was a Southern Baptist Convention church and a sister church of the other churches Jerry had served previously, it had minor operational differences when compared to the churches he had served on Sand Mountain. While the baseline ministries and missions of the churches were the same, the local environments surrounding each of the churches created specific needs for the individual churches. Whereas country churches were more relaxed and had fewer time constraints, city churches tended to operate on a stricter time schedule and they seemed to have more procedural guidelines. The crowded living conditions of the city communities surrounding the churches created a special set of opportunities for the pastor and church. In those situations, such simple things as visitation and other outreach programs must be efficiently handled within tight time constraints. Many times, the needs of urban dwellers differ from those of rural dwellers. Spiritual needs of both groups are usually very similar, but methods of dealing with them vary from location to location. With God's help, Brother Jerry Ross and the fine congregation of East Lake Baptist Church surmounted the particular situation there and built a successful ministry there. It was accomplished through prayer, patience, and perseverance.

The ministry at East Lake Baptist Church in Guntersville, Alabama was blessed richly by God. During that two-year ministry, several people came into the Christian fold and joined the church. A real highlight of that portion of Jerry Ross's ministry was the fact that two young men announced their call to preach during that time. The appearance and demeanor of one of them raised some eyebrows in the congregation of the church. He had experienced a rough life prior to his calling, and some of the results of that life were still evident in his physical appearance after his conversion. This led to some skepticism on the part of his

109

fellow parishioners. The sincerity and change in this young man's life soon erased that skepticism. Both of these men are now successfully pastoring churches. One of them, the Reverend Kerry Sims, is now serving as the pastor of Pilgrim's Rest Baptist Church near Geraldine, Alabama. It is interesting to note that Brother Jerry served as pastor of Pilgrim's Rest after he completed his ministry at East Lake Baptist Church. The other young man who answered God's call to preach during Jerry's East Lake ministry, Brother Gary Swords, is currently serving as pastor of Dixie Street Baptist Church in Albertville, Alabama. Both of these men have successful ministries that are lovingly blessed by the Heavenly Father. Brother Jerry maintains contact with both of them to this day and worships with them whenever he can.

Serving East Lake Baptist Church was a very rewarding experience for Brother Jerry Ross, and one during which God taught him many lessons and proceeded to expand his experience base. He has many fond memories of his work there and gives God all the credit for any progress that was there. After about two years, God lifted Jerry's burden for East Lake Baptist Church and he knew it was time to move to another work as he was led by God.

Following the leadership of the Heavenly Father, Jerry resigned as pastor of East Lake Baptist Church and awaited God's direction and leadership for his future work. Shortly thereafter, he was called to pastor Pilgrim's Rest Baptist Church near Geraldine, Alabama.

Brother Jerry approached his new assignment with an open mind that was fully attuned to God's wavelength. He knew that he would be facing a challenge that was different from any of the previous ones. As with his previous pastorates, he set out to establish a strong visitation program at Pilgrim's Rest. Jerry's philosophy is, and has always been, that one of the greatest works of a pastor is that of being actively in the field, visiting and witnessing in the community and inviting people to the church. In keeping with that philosophy, he began an aggressive visitation program at Pilgrim's Rest. Despite some misgivings about the program by some of the membership, Jerry and some of the other parishioners set out to visit in the community surrounding the church. They visited active members of the church as well as inactive members as they sought to learn of special needs in the community. They had a goal of ministering to those needs, in an effort to bring those folks into a greater fellowship with God and one another. An equally important goal was to reach sinners of the community and bring them into a saved relationship with Christ.

After the inception of the visitation program, Brother Jerry set out to visit an elderly man of the community who lived about a mile from the church. Some of the church members advised against going to visit the man. They knew he was a lost man, but they considered him somewhat of an arrogant recluse and one who did not welcome visitors, nor did he like to talk to them. Acting against that advice, Brother Jerry and some church members went to visit the man anyway. They found that the man was basically as the church members had described him. They had prayer with him and then left to visit others in the community. On later visits to the man and his wife, she made things right with the Lord and got saved and got into church. Shortly thereafter, the man's health began to deteriorate very rapidly and the family moved to Gadsden. For a period of time, Jerry did not hear from that family. More than two years later after Brother Jerry had accepted pastoral work at another church and had experienced a severe heart attack himself, the man sent him a message that lifted Brother Jerry's spirit in a glorious way. The man said, "Don't worry. I got saved. I know I am dying, but I'm going to heaven!" The rewarding thing was that the man sent the message two or three years after Brother Jerry's first visit to him and even after Jerry had been called to Aurora Baptist Church. Jerry feels strongly that God can come back and reward a willing servant for work that he did years before under His leadership. Jerry says, "All of us want to do a tangible Christian work and see the results then, but some of the work we do has no tangible results at the time. Many of the things we do have to be done with faith in Him. God may delay the results and time them according to His will." Jerry's experience here is the perfect example of what can be accomplished if we follow God's instructions and then wait patiently upon the Lord.

A second memorable event in Jerry's ministry at Pilgrim's Rest occurred during a visit to another home in the church community. He felt a distinct leadership of God to visit a certain home in the community, and fully trusting Him, made his desire for that visit known to the Visitation Committee. He was advised against making that visit, since the occupants of the home had not attended church for a long period of time and had a reputation for being unreceptive to visitors from the church. They were experiencing severe family difficulties and assorted other problems at the time and had withdrawn from any association with the community. Brother Jerry responded by saying, "Those are the very people who need Christ the most." Feeling very strongly that he should visit the family, Jerry prayed about the situation and then announced that he should go ahead with the visit. As it turned out, the church members' assessment of the family was wrong. The members of the family turned out to be very gracious hosts. Upon his arrival at the couple's home, Brother Jerry was cordially received and invited in for a visit. He said that he had never been treated any better or with more respect than that he experienced during that visit. During that and subsequent visits, he learned that the man had never been saved, and that although the wife had been saved, she was out of fellowship with God at the time. Although the man never accepted Christ during Brother Jerry's ministry at Pilgrim's Rest Church, he was receptive to having prayer during Jerry's visits to the home. The man's wife got back into church after making peace with God and her previously neglected and spurned Savior, Jesus Christ.

A third visitation experience at Pilgrim's Rest is still fresh on Brother Jerry's mind to this date and confirms his firm belief that a major part of a pastor's work is in the field. That particular situation developed prior to the commencement of the weekly visitation activities. The Visitation Committee had met at the church for prayer on a Tuesday night before visiting in the community. After having prayer, Brother Jerry asked those present that night if any of them had any burden for a special visit to some person in the community. He suggested the name of one man, a Mr. Reagan, who had been on his mind that day. Mr. Reagan did not know Jesus at the time, and Brother Jerry felt that the group should visit him. Mr. Reagan's son Danny suggested that it might not be a good time to visit his father. When none of the others present responded to Jerry's request for possible visitation objectives for that night, he said, "Let's go back and have prayer again and specifically ask God for directions on where we should visit tonight. Let's ask Him to burden someone's heart about a person we should visit tonight." At the conclusion of the fervent prayer, Brother Jerry asked if anyone had received any directions or burden from God during the prayer about any person they should visit that night. Brother Danny Reagan said with tears in his eyes, "Yes. I feel now that we should visit my daddy tonight."

With those specific directions from God, Brother Jerry and the group left the church immediately and made their way to the Reagan home. Upon arriving, the group went to the front. They heard someone frantically pacing the floor inside and, at the same time, making sounds that indicated that the person was in a state of stress. Brother Jerry knocked on the door, hoping all the while that everything was all right in the house. Mr. Reagan asked them in and appeared to be relieved that they had come to visit him that night. He was under heavy conviction at the time and the full realization of the consequences of being lost had dawned on him. Brother Jerry and the group shared the appropriate scriptures from the book of Romans with Mr. Reagan and explained the plan of salvation to him. They all knelt and prayed for Mr. Reagan to find Christ as his personal Savior. Mr. Reagan arose from the prayer, and joyously shouted, "I'm saved! I'm saved!"

The story of Mr. Reagan's salvation is a tribute to our loving God and is a prime example of what God will do when His children seek His directions and then follow them in faith. That incident vividly illustrates and confirms Brother Jerry Ross's conviction and belief that a major portion of a minister's work is in the field.

Once again and with God's ever-present help, Brother Jerry Ross had a successful ministry at Pilgrim's Rest. He had accepted the call to the church, knowing that there were some disagreements and minor difficulties among the members, but none that couldn't be solved with the application of some Christian love and understanding. With lots of prayer and patience, the church began to grow and work in harmony. After two years, Brother Jerry felt that his work at Pilgrim's Rest was done. He was grateful to God for bringing him through some rocky times during the early part of his ministry there. Jerry left Pilgrim's satisfied that he had completed the work he had been sent there to do. He thanked God for the opportunity of being there to work in a field with special needs and for His help and leadership during that work.

After a brief interlude, Brother Jerry answered the call to be the pastor of Aurora Baptist Church southwest of Boaz, Alabama on Alabama Highway 179. Aurora Baptist Church was a small church, but one filled with character and a history of dedicated service to God and the Aurora community. Jerry was overwhelmed with the reception he and his wife had received after he had answered Aurora Baptist's call. He welcomed the opportunity to work with a church, although very small, that was in harmony and in communion with God's will. He and Darlene were very impressed by the loving way that they were accepted into the Aurora Baptist family. They felt right at home in Aurora Baptist Church from the beginning and went directly to the work at hand, with Jerry delivering God's Word from the pulpit and visiting in the community as time allowed.

As was his custom when accepting and going on the field of a new work, Brother Jerry immediately began looking for a project for the church members of Aurora Baptist Church to work on together. In short order, he thought of several projects that the church members could work on together. The first project was one that required the services of the men of the church. It was an activity that required hard work and ingenuity. It was also dirty and had a strong and obnoxious odor. Brother Jerry and the men of the church decided to tackle the job of resealing the paved parking lot that served the church patrons. Their goal was to save some money for the church and at the same time to have some fun and fellowship and to enjoy the satisfaction that comes from successfully completing a job by working together.

The parking lot had been paved several years earlier, and after years of use, was in need of minor repairs and resealing. Brother Jerry had talked to the men of the church regarding the project and they were in agreement that the work needed to be done. Inexperienced as they were, the group met ahead of time and made plans for the project, and with the concurrence of the church, ordered all the materials needed for the project. Commercial contractors who normally do this work have spray equipment, material handling equipment, and other labor-saving devices. Brother Jerry and his group had none of those items, but they filled the gap with God's help, prayer, cooperation, ingenuity, determination, main strength, and plenty of hard work. Thus equipped, they tackled the job head on without any thoughts of failure.

The men of the church set about their work early on the appointed day. The sealer product for the job had been picked up in Oneonta, Alabama at an earlier time and was at the church and ready for use. The first task of the day was to sweep the parking lot and clear it of all dirt, pebbles, grass, and twigs. That need was quickly accomplished by the determined group and they moved on to the next step of the work with great anticipation. One of the first problems the group encountered was how to handle the fifty-five-gallon drums of sealer. The full drums weighed about 500 pounds and were filled with a thick black liquid that was sticky and very unpleasant to handle. Beside that, the drums of sealer were on trucks belonging to some of the men of the church, and to worsen matters, there was no forklift or other equipment to help unload the heavy drums of sealer material. At that point in the game, some good old "country boy" logic came into effect as God began to lead the receptive minds of Brother Jerry and the men and boys of the church as they put themselves to the task of sealing the parking lot.

The group of willing but inexperienced workers contemplated the problems before them and began to have serious doubts about their ability to solve them in a way that would produce a nice job. The drums were on trucks and they needed them on the ground. Once they were on the ground, and with no pump available, how did one get the sealer out of the drums? Then what was the best way to spread the foul-smelling material into a smooth, even coat on the surface of the parking lot? They approached the problems in an orderly fashion and dealt with them one at a time.

After mulling the drum unloading problem over in their minds, the men came up with a unique way of unloading the drums of material from the truck. They brought in a number of old tires and carefully placed them on the parking lot surface directly behind the end of the truck bed. There were multiple layers of tires immediately behind the truck. Then they tilted the full drums over into a horizontal position on the trucks and gingerly rolled them off the truck onto the tires. That simple drum unloading method worked surprisingly well and was employed several times by the determined group as they unloaded the drums at the actual point of need.

When the drums were on the ground, the next problem involved getting the sealant material out of the drum and onto the pavement of the parking lot. Once again, a simple solution was revealed to the men and boys doing the work. The thought occurred to some of the men that there was a way to do the needed job without any extra equipment. They reasoned, why not roll the drum along the pavement service until the bung was at the very top of the drum? Next, the bung plug would be loosened and removed, allowing a small amount of the sealant to run out.

115

With that in mind, they rolled the full drum of sealant to the starting point and removed the bung plug. Lo and behold, a small amount of the material ran out onto the pavement. Some of the boys and men spread the material evenly with mops. Others then rolled the drum slightly, discharging more material onto the pavement and the mopping procedure was repeated. That simple process was repeated until all the drums were empty and the job was complete. Without basic equipment and with the help of a merciful God, a group of determined men and boys completed a needed job at their church in record time and without mishap. Not only did they improve the looks of the church and its surroundings, but they also experienced a deep satisfaction in doing something together. Brother Jerry praised God for the project and the group of individuals, church members and non-members, who unselfishly gave of their time and support to a worthy project. He said that some of the participants in the project became members of Aurora Church as a result the project that allowed them to get to know church members.

One of those participants in the project, a young man, came into the church as a result of the sealing project. He had attended Aurora Baptist Church on a limited basis prior to the project, but had never taken any kind of active part in the church. Some of the men of the church stated that they had tried to talk to him and had witnessed to him on more than one occasion. The young man, on those rare times he came to church, would sit quietly in the congregation without speaking to anyone. The men had prayed for him and invited him to participate in church activities, to no avail. He came to the church on the appointed day and told Brother Jerry that he wanted to help with the project. His shyness and timid personality were very obvious to Brother Jerry. Seeing an opportunity to reach an errant sinner, Brother Jerry invited the young man to work with him that day. Brother Jerry talked to him and displayed a genuine interest in him as the day progressed. As the project got into full swing, the young fellow loosened up and began to ply Jerry with questions and to discuss the project in general terms. Jerry responded, answered his questions, and gained the boy's trust. During the day, he witnessed to the young man and asked him to visit the church on Sunday. Brother Jerry was very grateful and thankful to God for two things that had occurred that day: First, the parking lot was repaired and secondly, a soul was led back into the church fold. The young man began to attend church and take part in the activities. Some time later, he paid Brother Jerry a high compliment. During a service, the young man came into the church and walked to the front of the church and then asked Jerry if he could sit by him. Brother Jerry was touched by the unsolicited vote of confidence displayed by the young man. He once again thanked God for the unique opportunity he had been given to help change a life.

The happenings of that day bolstered Brother Jerry's long-held belief that a pastor has duties apart from filling the pulpit. He will be the first to say that the pastor must fill the pulpit and preach the gospel, but that he also must spend time in the community, visiting and inviting people to church. He is firmly convinced by God that part of his duties as God's called representative must be to conceive and promote church activities that lead people to work together and combine their strengths and efforts in service to God. Brother Jerry says that people have been won to Christ by prayer, by the preached Word, by Christian testimonies, by observance of Christ-filled lives, and by the perfect work of God acting through the Holy Spirit. The pavement-sealing project showed clearly that people could be won through projects involving hard work. Jerry spent the day working with the young man as a partner and succeeded in gaining his confidence, thereby showing that God "works in strange ways, His wonders to perform."

Another community-oriented project Brother Jerry proposed and led at Aurora Baptist Church was an event called "Old-fashioned Day." Although Aurora Baptist was a good church and one blessed with a dedicated membership, the fact was that it was very small and one that needed to grow. Recognizing that fact, Brother Jerry sought a project that would draw participation from the entire community. The Aurora community was a rather tight-knit but not outgoing community group. Jerry, strongly believing that the pastor and church should be active members of the host community, set out to bring that state of affairs to life. With the help of a few church members, he set out to achieve two goals. The first was to lead sinners to Christ and hopefully grow a stronger church. The second goal was to introduce the church to the community and at the same time involve the church and its influence in the affairs of the community.

The church membership supported Brother Jerry's idea, and together they set out to plan the day. It would be a day of worship in the old-time

117

way, complete with "dinner on the grounds." The entire Aurora community was notified about the affair and issued invitations to the function. It was suggested that everyone dress in period clothes: sun bonnets, long dresses, and aprons for the ladies; overalls, white or colored shirts with ties, and hats for the men. The boys would emulate their fathers in dress and the girls would copy their mothers' attire. All were asked to bring basket lunches for everyone to share. The men and women of the church were to prepare the church and grounds for the affair. When that work started, many community members pitched in and helped with the chores.

The big day arrived and the crowd started gathering at the church well before the announced starting time. By the time the program began, the house was packed with happy people looking forward to a day of worship, fellowship, good food, and community involvement. The worship service was conducted as if it was taken from a page of history. After the preliminaries of old-time hymn singing, testimony, and prayer, Brother Jerry, resplendent in his overalls, white shirt, and red tie, delivered the message God had given him. Later, the entire crowd enjoyed a bountiful lunch spread beneath the stately oaks and pines surrounding the church.

The day was a resounding success and one that is remembered to this day. It was a "shot in the arm" for Aurora Baptist Church and one that served to draw a good community closer together. Brother Jerry says that community and church members still talk to him about the affair.

Brother Jerry had been at Aurora Baptist a year when God told him to give up the church. Those directions came as a shock to him. He had seen the attendance figures for Sunday morning worship services of the Aurora Baptist Church grow from fifteen or twenty in attendance to one hundred or more. The church was in harmony; the fellowship was great; church programs were going well and finally, the church was still growing. Jerry and Darlene were truly enjoying their service to Aurora Baptist Church and were getting blessed at every turn. When he told Darlene of the instructions he had received from on high, they had a lengthy discussion about the matter. After all the discussion, often filled with alternatives, Jerry knew that he must obey God's instructions, and accordingly, he resigned the pastorate of Aurora Baptist Church during the next Sunday morning worship service. With sad hearts, Jerry and Darlene left Aurora, not knowing where they were to go next or what they should do.

About a month after leaving Aurora Baptist, Jerry was invited to preach at Pineview First Congregational Methodist Church near Howellton, Alabama on a Sunday night. He took his scripture from 2 Corinthians, chapter 4 and chose as his text "But Not…" as found in verses 8 and 9. In his opening remarks about the message, he stated that this one could be the last one that he would get to enjoy delivering. Jerry delivered the message, and in closing, he once again stated that the message might be his last. He did not really know why he made those particular remarks or why he felt the way he did. A strange foreboding feeling had been overshadowing him for several days and continued to fill him with uncertainty as that Sunday passed. Was it a premonition or was it a subtle warning from God that something unusual was about to happen? The answer would become apparent as the events of the following Tuesday began to unfold.

Tuesday, July 20, 1999 proved to be a fateful day for Jerry Ross. Jerry did not sleep well the Monday night before, and as a result, awakened very early on Tuesday morning. He had a feeling of dread pressing on him at the time and he went for a walk around his house in an effort to allay his concerns about the events facing him that day. He sought God's help and solace in sincere prayer during the walk. God gave him peace in his heart during that walk and he returned to the house with calm assurance in his heart, ready to face the challenges of the day. Feeling better about the unknowns he was facing later that day, Brother Jerry and Darlene, in the company of son Daryl and his wife then departed for Birmingham, Alabama.

The day's activities in Birmingham began with an appointment with Dr. Jerry Chandler of Montclair Hospital, now known as Trinity Hospital. The purpose of the appointment was to let Dr. Chandler deal with a problem that had arisen with two stents that had been previously installed in critical locations around Jerry Ross's heart. Jerry reported to the hospital early on that day and completed all the pre-operation procedures that had to be done before the actual surgical procedure. One of those procedures was a preliminary meeting with Dr. Chandler. Upon meeting with Jerry, Dr. Chandler noted that he was quieter than usual and was not kidding as he usually did. Dr. Chandler inquired of Jerry, "How do you feel? I notice that something is different."

Jerry responded, "I feel good. Let's get on with it." Jerry was then ready for the surgery, with the exception of one thing. That exception was

119

removed when Jerry Ross and Dr. Chandler, a dedicated Christian, had prayer before the actual procedure began. They placed the whole thing in His hands and asked for His blessing upon the operation. With all the preliminaries completed, Jerry was moved to the operating room for the surgery to begin.

Once Jerry was in Trinity Hospital's catheterization laboratory, Dr. Chandler began to perform the initial steps of the catheterization procedure. Because he was not heavily anesthetized, Jerry was aware of what was going on and was able to talk to Dr. Chandler as the operation began. They exchanged very brief remarks and then, almost instantly and without warning, Jerry suffered a very severe heart attack and passed out and slipped into a deep coma that lasted for many days. Immediately after he passed out, Jerry was rushed into the operating room for additional life-saving procedures including surgery. With all possible haste and almost within minutes, the doctors performed emergency open-heart surgery on Jerry Ross, during which two bypasses were made on clogged arteries at his heart. Following the surgery and other heroic measures employed to save his life, the condition of his heart and lungs was such that his chest had to be left open for three days before closure was possible.

While he was in that deep coma for a lengthy period following the heart attack and emergency surgery, he had an out-of-body and near-death experience that would be the ultimate peak of his relationship with God; the absolute pinnacle of his numerous Christian experiences that had been so much a part of his life for several years. Jerry Ross has absolutely no memory of anything that occurred in the physical world during that period. He has no memories whatsoever about his treatments during that time or the valiant and heroic efforts of Dr. Chandler and his staff to keep him alive. He does, however, have extremely vivid memories of the things his soul experienced during the time he was in a coma. He says that all the words in his vocabulary, indeed all the words known to man, are grossly inadequate to describe the beauty he saw, the peace he felt, and the words and singing he heard.

The comatose state following the heart attack and surgery lasted for days, during which Jerry showed no response to anything or anyone. Jerry has learned since that, as he was beginning to come out of the deep coma, the team of doctors decided to keep him in an induced coma for the next several days because of the extremely weakened condition of his heart as

120

it was healing after the heart attack. The induced coma allowed complete rest for Jerry's body and minimized the load and strain on his ailing heart. There were some brief times during that period when Jerry would open his eyes and show some very fleeting indications of alertness.

Brother Jerry's description of his out-of-body experience during that period immediately following his heart attack is astounding. Having experienced some minor chest pains in the days preceding his visit to Birmingham, he recalls some severe pains at the time he passed out. Jerry says that in his dreamlike state at the time, it felt as if a refrigerator was flat across his chest and that it seemed to be held down with straps. The weight became heavier for a while and the pain more intense. The pain inside him became so intense that he felt as if his chest would burst. In addition to that, Jerry remembers that he was getting very cold and that the pain increased dramatically as he became colder. Then it felt as if he was trying to rise from the operating table, but it seemed that the straps were still doing their best to hold him down. It seemed to him that he had to be freed from the restraints and weights that were holding him on the table. Finally, the restraints and weights that held him could hold him no longer and he began to rise to a height that he describes as being about ceiling level of the operating room. At that point, the pain began to subside and he began to feel warm again. Jerry then rose a little higher and looked down upon the scene unfolding below him. Without realizing what it was at first, he saw an operating table surrounded by people, all of whom were feverishly working on a prone body lying before them. Then Jerry realized that God was letting him see the scene in the operating room that he had been moved into after his life-threatening heart attack. Following that, and in a startling revelation, he knew that the body he was looking down on was his own seemingly lifeless body as it drew the undivided attention of all those scurrying around the operating table below. God also revealed to him that his spiritual body and soul were about to leave the damaged physical body. An indescribable peace began to envelop Jerry and he felt the loving, powerful, and merciful presence of the Lord as his spirit began to ascend to greater heights. As he moved higher, he felt the presence of people who were there to lead and guide him and to help him along the way. As he made his way along, Jerry saw what appeared to be a beautiful field of wheat. All the plants, untold numbers of them, were the same height and color and loaded with grain. When the wind gently blew on them, they all obediently leaned in unison with the direction of the breezes, thereby creating a scene reminiscent of gentle ripples moving across a smooth body of water. The plants obeyed the influence of the breezes, regardless of their direction. As Jerry recalls the scene, he says, "Everything was fitly framed together."

As Jerry and his party left the wheat field scene and moved on, a train came by and stopped for them. Jerry boarded the train and rode for a short time, then left it. He began to walk and then began to see a glow in the distance. As he hurried toward the glow, he heard voices as they praised and worshipped the source of the brilliant glow. As Jerry got closer to the glow, he could see the back side of a man who was surrounded by the glow. He was in a sitting position and was facing all those souls who were worshipping and praising Him. He was rejoicing with them and His wonderful love and mercy seemed to radiate from Him to all those gathered around Him. Viewing that wonderful scene with indescribable awe, Jerry pointed at the figure and asked, "Is that Him?" The worshippers and all the angels began to praise and worship Him all the more and then spoke in mighty chorus, "That's Him! Oh! That's Him! That's Him!" Jerry says of the meeting, "I didn't get to see Him from the front, but I did get to see Him from the back side. I will never forget the magnificent and glorious scene I saw, nor will I ever forget the peace I felt at the time." Recalling the wonderful incident and glimpse of his Savior, Jerry says today, "I wish I could find words to explain how I felt. The next thing I knew, there was the wheat field again."

Back at the previously seen wheat field, with its fantastic beauty and order, Jerry got back on the train and it began to move away from the wheat field. The train soon stopped at another location and the conductor, whom Jerry did not recognize, said, "If you don't get off now, you are gone for eternity!" The next thing Jerry knew was that his oldest son Daryl was slapping him on the hand and saying, "Daddy, wake up! Daddy, wake up! Can you talk? Can you move?"

After all those days in a coma, Jerry awoke back into a world that he had almost left after the heart attack and its resulting complications. While he was comatose, either by the effect of the heart attack or by inducement, he suffered many other problems. During that time, he developed pneumonia and other lung problems, experienced difficulty breathing on several occasions during the recovery, and dealt with mobility problems brought about by nerve damage. Jerry was in and out of the coronary care unit more than once in his recovery. His status was extremely critical for a number of days, and the healing process was very slow and beset by reverses. After a long period of time, Jerry's body slowly gained strength and his heart recovered enough for him to breathe on his own. There were long sessions of therapy to help him regain the use of his arms and legs so he could walk, feed himself, and tend to his needs. Jerry was finally released from the hospital after forty-two days and allowed to return home.

The response of Jerry's family, friends, and members of churches he had pastored, as well as members of sister churches, was nothing short of overwhelming during his sickness and recovery. Jerry's wife Darlene kept a log of calls and visits that he received during his stay in the hospital. The log is a magnificent testament of the love, friendship, concern, and high esteem all those people have for Jerry. The log reveals that he received 1,025 calls or visits during his hospitalization. That is an average of more than twenty-four per day. Jerry, in his modesty, says that he was undeserving of such an outpouring of love, but he is thankful for the concern of his friends and family. Most of all, he gives God the glory and praise for his miraculous recovery. Although Jerry has limited heart function, he knows that God brought him through the very depths of the valley of the shadow of death and that He had a purpose for it.

After returning home and gaining some strength, Jerry felt that he wanted to keep preaching. After trying it, he fully realized that he did not have the strength or stamina to do it. Dr. Chandler, with his complete knowledge of Jerry's health situation, advised him not to attempt to preach because of the strain that preaching would place on his severely weakened heart. God, having once again saved Jerry for a purpose, opened up a hospital and nursing home visitation ministry for him. As his health has permitted, Jerry has been a faithful visitor to hospitals and nursing homes. Although his health places restrictions on the scope of his ministry, Jerry continues to actively serve God in a visitation ministry, by regular church attendance and by mentoring young ministers.

The Jerry Ross Ministerial Philosophy

The Reverend Jerry Ross has had a very unusual and interesting ministry since he answered God's call and entered the ministry. In his work in God's field for the past few years, he has been blessed to work as the pastor of several churches. As a result, he has encountered variations in the missions and modes of worship of those churches. While all of the churches soundly embraced the basic tenets of the Southern Baptist Church as outlined by the guidelines of the Baptist Faith and Message document, actual services and church operational procedures employed by the individual churches varied a great deal from church to church. Rules adopted by the Southern Baptist Convention allow a goodly amount of freedom in the establishment of the constitution and bylaws of the individual churches. Those documents, though crafted to meet the needs of the individual church and to provide guidelines for the conduction of church's business, can never be contrary to the teachings and direction of the Holy Bible or the rules established by the Southern Baptist Convention. As Jerry's pastoral ministry progressed through service in several churches, he observed the freedom of worship and service to God and mankind enjoyed by sister churches within the groups, small to large, that exist in the Southern Baptist Convention.

Reverend Jerry Ross firmly believes that a pastor's highest priority in serving God and a church is that of filling the pulpit as one of God's chosen messengers and delivering the message of the Good News of the Gospel of a Risen Savior to a lost world. One of his guidelines for that work is found in 2 Timothy 4:2, where the Apostle Paul is instructing Timothy with these words: "Preach the word; be instant in season, out of season; reprove, rebuke, exhort with all long suffering and doctrine." Brother Jerry learned early in his ministry that as pastor, he must be in constant touch with God through prayer, meditation, and study while constantly seeking God's leadership and instructions concerning what he should do and say in any given situation. He is a firm believer in the Apostle Paul's instructions to Timothy in 2 Timothy 3:15, where he says, "Study to show thyself approved unto God, a workman that needeth not to be ashamed, rightly dividing the word of truth." Another favorite foundation scripture of Jerry's is found in John 14:14, where Jesus says, "If ye shall ask anything in my name, I will do it." Those two verses are the very foundation of his ministerial philosophy. Brother Jerry has always had complete faith in God that He will provide the inspiration and resources for the messages He asks Jerry to deliver. Jerry fully believes in the Great Commission as Jesus Christ delivered it in Matthew 28 and that it should issue forth from established churches to the uttermost parts of the world.

As the years of his ministry have passed, Jerry has also found that several factors shape the missions and operation of the member churches within the Missionary Baptist Associations. The presence of those factors, when coupled with guidelines of the Baptist Faith and Message, the local church's constitution and bylaws, and the preached Word, have served to broaden and solidify the principles of Brother Jerry's ministerial philosophy.

Brother Jerry found that the factors that often influence the formation of a church's order of service and mission vary from location to location. Generally speaking, he learned that urban churches, as a general rule, are likely to employ more rigid time schedules for services than their rural counterparts. He also found that the missions of the individual churches, as well as their rites of worship, are most often influenced by the nature and physical makeup of the individual church communities themselves. Another factor that often influences the operation of the church is the specific need or needs of that particular church community. Jerry Ross learned early in his ministry that he should always do his best in his pastorates to conform as closely as possible to the mode of operation and established pattern of worship of the church that he was serving at the time. Although that philosophy added an additional dimension of study and investigation to the requirements of his service as pastor of a given church, it paid handsome dividends as the ministry progressed.

Early in his ministry, even at his first pastorate at Butler Baptist Church, Brother Jerry learned that there needs to be some device developed within the church that will act as a catalyst in drawing the church members together into a state of cohesiveness and commitment to a common cause. He learned that those devices or projects could be small or large and that they should serve to fulfill a specific need of the church. During his ministry, the programs conceived by Brother Jerry and his congregations ranged from a simple church visitation program, such as that begun at Butler Baptist Church, to a major repair and update of Pilgrim's Rest Baptist; they ranged from an "Old-fashioned Day" to a major paving project for the parking lot at Aurora Baptist Church. They also ranged from the establishment of a cemetery at Corinth Baptist Church to a major visitation program at East Lake Baptist Church. All of those projects complemented the preached Word delivered from the pulpit and served to bring the members of the various churches into a state of unity as they worked together to achieve a given goal for the church's benefit. Jerry learned that parishioners who were drawn together by the common bond of a worthwhile church improvement project tended to be drawn more closely together in corporate worship services. He also learned that the project must be carefully and thoroughly explained to the church group, with special emphasis on the need at hand. Brother Jerry is quick to point out that strong-armed unilateral tactics will not work in the presentation of a given project to the church body. He states that the church members are much more likely to buy into a project if they fully understand it and if it is presented to them in Christian love. They must understand that it is for the glory of God and for the promotion of His cause and not to bolster the egos of mankind.

Additionally, Reverend Jerry Ross's ministerial philosophy recommends strongly that a pastor establish a Christian identity and presence in the church community. He says that a pastor should be an example of Christian virtue and principle in his church community and one who seeks out and ministers to special needs found in the community. Over the years, Brother Jerry has found many areas of service outside the walls of the churches he has been privileged to serve as pastor. Visitation of local and area nursing homes, hospitals, assisted-living facilities, and retirement homes has been a special part of his ministry and still is to this time. Even though poor health has forced him to give up his pastoral work, he still visits in those areas as his health permits.

Brother Jerry Ross feels that God's call to the ministry is a lifetime commitment and one that is not to be taken lightly. He knows that there comes a time in every minister's life when age or health will force him to give up an active pastorate, but he also knows that God will open the doors to other areas of service.

Jerry Ross is thankful for the opportunities that God has given him over the years, and will be eternally grateful for having a part in God's special work. He gives God all the praise and glory for anything that was accomplished in his ministry. Jerry readily admits that God was patient with him and protected him and brought him through many dangerous and trying situations, even when he was rebelling against God's clear call to repentance. Jerry Ross says it all was "only through grace" freely given by a loving God that he was able to turn his life around and become a worker in the Heavenly Father's field. With genuine modesty and heartfelt thanks, Jerry says, "To God be the glory!"

Finally, Brother Jerry Ross urges the readers of this book to promptly answer any call to service that God may send to them and, by doing so, avoid the plague and heartbreak of wasted years. His prayer for you, the reader, is that God will richly bless your life, witness, and any special ministry that He gives you. Jerry wants everyone to know that serving Jesus really pays.

Printed in the United States
144768LV00004B/8/P